Contributing Editor: Don Gardner

Edited by Brad Shirley

Cover Image: John Tobin/Tobinphoto.com

Visit www.booksurge.com to order additional copies.

Like the Eagle

Pastor Leonard Gardner

2008

Like the Eagle

CONTENTS

Introduction ix

Chapter 1—Like the Eagle in Vision 1

Chapter 2—Like the Eagle in Reproduction and
Maturation. 23

Chapter 3—Like the Eagle in Diet. 35

Chapter 4—Like the Eagle in Renewal 47

Chapter 5—Like the Eagle in Overcoming
Storms and Serpents. 57

Chapter 6—Like the Eagle in Commitment 73

Chapter 7—Becoming Like the Eagle. 79

INTRODUCTION

Of all the creatures on earth, the eagle stands out as among the most noble, majestic, fierce, and awe-inspiring. It is used as a symbol by many companies and nations because of its amazing attributes such as its mastery of the awesome force of the wind, its beauty in flight, and its strength in battle. It has remarkable vision and hunting prowess, and it flies at incredible heights. The eagle's strength, speed and majesty give it dominion over all other birds and the authority to "rule the heavens." The eagle is undoubtedly the king of birds. It can be difficult to find enough superlatives to describe the eagle.

The Bible refers to the eagle, its actions, and its attributes in a number of scriptures. Though the eagle is a part of a family of birds which includes 300 species, when Scripture makes reference to the eagle, it is referring to the Golden Eagle or the Imperial Eagle, which are very similar. The word imperial means "having supreme authority."

Learning from the Eagle

The Bible is full of similes that show us a natural pattern by which we can see a spiritual truth. Isaiah 40:30-31 declares, "Even the youths shall faint and be weary, and the young men shall utterly fall: But they that wait upon the LORD shall renew their strength; they shall mount up with wings as eagles; they shall run, and not be weary; and they shall walk, and not faint." In this Scripture passage, there is a simile that reveals to us powerful truth about God's design for the way a Christian should live. Often times, as in this case, the word "like" or "as" is used as a figure of speech by writers to show a comparison of two unlike things. "They that wait upon the Lord...shall mount up with wings 'as' eagles." Here, God is showing us that there are characteristics of the eagle (in particular, the Golden Eagle) that we too can possess in our lives.

Romans 8:29-30 states, "For whom he did foreknow, he also did predestinate to be conformed to the image of his Son, that he might be the firstborn among many brethren. Moreover whom he did predestinate, them he also called: and whom he called, them he also justified: and whom he justified, them he also glorified." God's plan always has been for us to be conformed to the image of His son. Everything that the Holy Spirit does in our lives is to help us become more like Jesus.

Careful study of the Word of God leads us to conclude that similes are frequently employed to compare the characteristics of natural things (i.e. sheep, eagles, etc.) with spiritual things. Through this, God is showing us characteristics that He Himself possesses as the Creator of all things. Nothing was created that was not first a characteristic of the Creator. As the Holy Spirit moves in our lives and we yield to His loving hand, He molds and shapes us to be more like Jesus. Under the guidance of the Holy Spirit, men wrote of natural things in the Bible, like the eagle, to point out characteristics that God wants us to possess.

In a born again believer's life there are key components which are important to our spiritual growth and our walk with God. In this book we will make comparisons between the attributes of the eagle and the character of a believer. We are, in many ways, to be "like the eagle" in our Christian lives. In this book, we will understand how God wants us to be like the eagle in the sense of having clear vision and focus for our lives. We will learn that we should be like the eagle with regard to our "diet," meaning what we allow into our hearts and minds. We will learn that we should be like the eagle with regard to the way we learn, grow, and mature in order to become strong and effective in our Christian life. We will see the importance of being renewed like the eagle and what that means to us on a daily basis. We will learn that the eagle and the born again believer were both made to overcome all the storms and enemy attacks that we face in life. Finally, we will learn that the eagle is a tremendous example of commitment, a characteristic that is lacking in the world today, and how we too can be like the eagle in that area.

He Makes Us New

The eagle flies thousands of feet into the air. Airline pilots have reported seeing eagles at altitudes as high as 5,000 feet. The eagle is unique, superior in its species, and capable of amazing things. It is no ordinary bird. Similarly, we must understand and recognize that God has made each of us unique, and we are mighty through Him. Philippians 4:13 declares, "I can do all things through Christ which strengtheneth me." Many of the characteristics of the eagle can be applied to our everyday lives. That is God's desire for all of us. We are His creation, and we are intended to be majestic and mighty. That is how God sees us.

Unfortunately, for many of us, our perception of ourselves does not coincide with God's view of us. It is imperative that we, as born again believers, see ourselves a brand new person, because II Corinthians 5:17 declares, "Therefore, if anyone is in Christ, he is a new creation; the old has gone, the new has come!" (NIV) The starting point is to recognize the transformation that occurred when we accepted Jesus Christ as Lord of our life. *He makes us new!*

Frequently, our problem is that we hold on to our old ways and thoughts. We have been "conditioned" by our life before

Christ to see ourselves in a certain light. You may have had abusive parents, or parents that did not affirm you as a valuable person. You may have been through a divorce or bankruptcy. Perhaps you have been rejected, or addicted to some substance or habit. It is imperative as we study the eagle that you let go of the past and acknowledge that you are a new person and a new creation in Christ. God sees you through very different lenses than the ones through which you see yourself and the lenses through which other people perceive you. Have you ever put on someone else's glasses whose prescription was vastly different than yours? Your vision is blurry, unclear, and objects can be unrecognizable and undistinguishable.

See the New You

As a believer in Christ, you must allow the Holy Spirit to help you, by faith, to accept the truths that the Word of God says about you. It is like putting on new glasses—His glasses. It may take some time to see the new you, but the truth is what *God* says about you. <u>Don't accept what your *circumstances* say, or what *others* say, but instead accept what *He* says.</u> I encourage you to make a list of "old" things with which you no longer want to be identified. Most people can come up with such a list quickly because we have a tendency to recognize the negative things about ourselves. We can readily list our hurts and pains, things that have seemed unfair, things that made us angry, our sins and failures, our bad habits, and the mistakes we wish we had never made.

After you make that list, copy II Corinthians 5:17 and post that Scripture verse where you can see it every morning. "Therefore, if anyone is in Christ, he is a new creation; the old has gone, the new has come!" (NIV) Now, take your list and tear it into pieces or run it through a shredder. Do it as a symbolic act of forgetting the past and not living there any longer. This is not denial of the pain or sins of the past, but rather simply recognizing that the forgiveness of Christ has made you new. He sees you as forgiven, powerful, mighty, and capable of amazing things. As you journey into the incredible world of the eagle in the pages of this book, open your eyes to the truth that you are becoming a renewed, mature, and incredible person in Christ. He sees you as strong, powerful, beautiful, and majestic. . .like the eagle!

CHAPTER I

Like the Eagle in Vision

Job 39:27-29 declares, "Is it at your command that the eagle mounts up and makes his nest on high? On the cliff he dwells and lodges, upon the rocky crag, an inaccessible place. From there he spies out food; His eyes see *it* from afar." (NASB) Please note the last phrase, "...his eyes see it from afar." "Eagle-Eye" is an expression that is used to describe people that have the ability to see, notice, or identify things that others miss. This could also describe the eagle, because it has the keenest vision of any bird. In fact, the Golden Eagle can see a rabbit from over two miles away. For example, when an eagle flies at an altitude of over 10,000 feet, it cannot only visually identify, but also focus upon, something as small as a rabbit.

There are two important elements which give the eagle its astounding vision: 1) a double set of eyelids, and 2) tissues within the eyes called pectens. As we will discover, the second set of eyelids allows the eagle to stare directly into the sun, and the pectens are a built-in homing device for the eagle. We will draw spiritual analogies from these natural wonders as we learn to develop spiritual vision akin to the eagle's natural vision.

Vision Determines Direction

Vision is imperative for every Christian because *vision determines direction*. Proverbs 29:18 says, "Where there is no vision, the people perish." The Hebrew word translated "perish" does not refer to physical death, but rather to people who lack direction, are undisciplined, and tend to cast off restraint in order to "do their own thing." Merriam Webster's Dictionary defines "vision" as "the act or power of imagination; mode of seeing or conceiving; unusual discernment or foresight."

Many people do not keep their vision focused on where they are going, in natural circumstances as well as spiritual ones. Have you ever seen someone driving a car while reading a map or dialing a cell phone? Attempting to multitask while driving can produce dangerous or even deadly results, because it diverts the person's vision away from the road and from their destination. If their vision is removed from the road, it is likely that their vehicle will head in a direction that isn't safe or wasn't planned. Vision determines direction!

Likewise, having a clear vision in life—knowing where we want to go and keeping our eyes fixed on the destination—is important to prevent us from wasting time, missing God's purpose, getting sidetracked, or pursuing fruitless endeavors. It is good to have a general idea of where we are headed in life, but God wants us to have a clear vision. Helen Keller once stated, "The only thing worse than being blind is having sight but no vision." Do you have a vision for your future? God is a God of vision and direction. The Bible contains several accounts of people to whom God gave a vision and specific direction. Abraham, Moses, Paul, and of course Jesus are excellent examples of people who had a clear vision and pursued their God-given direction with all of their hearts.

In addition to a clear vision, we must have "focus." Focus helps us to fix our eyes on exactly what we need to do in order to reach our destination and fulfill the vision that we have in our heart. Someone that starts a business typically has a vision for what they want to accomplish. They have a vision of what product or service the business will provide, how it will be structured, and whom it will serve. They develop a business plan and work hard to implement it. This requires a daily <u>focus</u> on that vision for the businessperson to avoid distraction and continue to move toward his or her goals. Likewise, as Christians, we must keep our vision focused daily on God's plan and purpose for our lives so that we will not be distracted.

Staring at the Son

Eagles have two sets of eyelids. One set is used during flight, or for observation from its nest (Job 39:29). The second set of eyelids allows the eagle to stare directly into the sun without damaging its eyes. It allows the eagle to use the sun as a point of orientation, a landmark as to where it is flying.

As a Christian, our focus should be on Christ. The eagle is equipped and created to stare at the sun. Similarly, God created us to stare (remain focused upon) the Son—Jesus Christ. Hebrews 12:2 states, "Looking unto Jesus the author and finisher of our faith; who for the joy that was set before him endured the cross, despising the shame, and is set down at the right hand of the throne of God." This is how we gain "eagle-eye" vision in our walk with Christ. First and foremost, we must keep our focus on Jesus. Many Christians spend a lot of time focusing on someone else's vision. *Your* vision begins to be formed in *your* heart as *you* keep *your* focus, staring intently at the Son! It is through the everyday focus on Jesus the Son that we find direction for the future. If we focus on the circumstances around us, we may become discouraged and distracted. Through His work on the cross, Jesus provided us with an open door to talk directly with God. We no longer need an intermediary to talk to Him. Scripture clearly invites us to communicate personally with God. Hebrews 4:15-16 declares, "For we have not an high priest which cannot be touched with the feeling of our infirmities; but was in all points tempted like as we are, yet without sin. Let us therefore come boldly unto the throne of grace, that we may obtain mercy, and find grace to help in time of need."

One of the greatest truths of God's Word is that Jesus, the Son of God, became flesh (the incarnation). He walked in our shoes. He lived a sinless life. However, the Bible declares in Hebrews 4:15 that "He was in all points tempted like as we." We are not praying to a God that does not understand our struggles. Jesus felt those struggles on earth—rejection, temptation, betrayal, and even hatred. He experienced it all. When we speak to Jesus, He understands what we are battling!

Many times people feel like they cannot approach God with their "petty struggles." Some people don't even pray because they feel unworthy, but God wants us to come to Him with all of our needs. He has given us the capability to stare directly into the face of His Son! This is how vision is birthed. We begin to see things that God desires to reveal to us as we pray and study His Word. As we spend time focusing on Jesus, we begin to get a broader vision, one that is not just about ourselves, but also about others. (See II Corinthians 3:18.)

Spend Time with God

Psalm 16:11 declares, "Thou wilt shew me the path of life: in thy presence is fullness of joy; at thy right hand there are pleasures for evermore." God wants to show us the path of life, and this scripture tells us that it comes from being in His presence where He can talk with us and show us what path to take. We should talk to God about every decision, concern, and issue we face. He cares and wants to show us which way to go. Proverbs 3:5-6 encourages us to "Trust in the LORD with all thine heart; and lean not unto thine own understanding. In all thy ways acknowledge him, And he will direct thy paths." Many of us have heard this scripture often, but I wonder how many of us really inquire of the Lord in "all our ways?" We may not always see the "total" vision that we want to see. We may not see how everything will turn out, but staring at the Son and being in His presence will result in an increased vision for ourselves, our family, and our future.

It is amazing that the Lord gave the eagle the ability to stare directly into the sun. By doing so, the eagle can find direction and still hunt for food to meet its daily needs. Likewise, we as believers have the ability to focus our attention on the Son. By doing so, we will also find direction because He will guide us in every decision that we need to make. The eagle can stare at the sun, and it always informs him of his present location. Likewise, by keeping our focus on Jesus we will always know where we are. Because the eagle was created with the second set of eyelids that enable him to look into the sun, he is never blinded. Due to the work of Jesus on the cross we can look directly into His Word and approach His throne. When unexpected things come our way, we are not blindsided by them, because we know where we are and upon Whom we are focused. We are not lost. We may have encountered a distraction, but we have not lost our vision.

To establish and gain a vision in our life we must set a daily time to focus on the Son. We can "stare at the Son" through worship, by spending time in His Word, and by simply walking and talking with the Lord. In the world there are many things to "look at" and by which we can be easily distracted. Perhaps one of the most difficult things to do is to be still (quiet, alone, peaceful) and focus on Him.

You may have experienced a time in which incredible distractions and diversions have caused your focus to be on other things. This may have affected your vision and perhaps even given you a loss of direction in life. You may have lost sight of the destination that you were pursuing. Perhaps you are a leader, a pastor, a business owner, or a husband trying to bring direction to your family. *To recover your vision, stare at the Son!*

Fixed and Focused

In this chapter, I have referred to the word "focus" many times. We learned that the eagle can stare directly into the sun and can also see a rabbit from two miles away. These are more than just amazing facts. The eagle's example can bring us incredible revelation which we can apply in our daily walk with the Lord. Focus is something that we must learn to faithfully practice in our lives. Psalm 108:1-5 declares, "O God, my heart is fixed; I will sing and give praise, even with my glory. Awake, psaltery and harp: I myself will awake early. I will praise thee, O LORD, among the people: and I will sing praises unto thee among the nations. For thy mercy is great above the heavens: and thy truth reacheth unto the clouds. Be thou exalted, O God, above the heavens: and thy glory above all the earth."

The Hebrew word translated "fixed" means "faithfulness, fastened, firm, fitted, ready, right, set, be stable, establish, stand, or tarry." Webster's Dictionary tells us that the verb form of this word means "to converge" or "to concentrate attention on an effort for a significant length of time."

These two words, "fixed" and "focused," are very similar. I believe that David was saying in Psalm 108:1-5 that his heart—his vision—was fixed on the Lord. Please note that David first sets his focus in the morning. "I myself will awake early." He in effect is saying, "At the start of the day, before anything else can distract me, I am going to set my heart and my focus on the Lord." This is critical to daily success and progress in our walk with the Lord. Many people struggle to get out of bed, stumble to the coffee pot and start to think about all the "to do's" that will require their time and attention that day.

David had a secret that I believe is often ignored, and because it is ignored, it hinders us from learning how to focus and stay fixed and firm. Many people say, "I am not a morning person." Mornings may not be the best time for your primary Bible study, but I believe that it is scriptural to give the Lord attention in the morning. Take time to talk with Him, spending a few moments in the Bible and getting your heart and mind focused and fixed on God. Eagles often hunt in the morning. As the sun rises the eagle is focused on what it needs for the day. What we need for the day is help from the Lord! It is important that we tune into His voice, bring our concerns to Him, and ask Him to help us through the day and give us wisdom. We should begin our day by acknowledging the Lord and inviting Him to guide us and lead us (Proverbs 3:5, John 16:13). Jesus taught us to pray, "Give us this day our daily bread." (Matthew 6:11) We need time with God daily!

Up and Down

This world is filled with many distractions. In the course of a normal morning, before work, many people watch the news, check the stock market, engage in conversations, read the paper, and listen to the radio on the way to work. Once they are in front of the computer at work, simply checking unread emails can lead them on a 45-minute diversion from what they planned to accomplish that day! Many things compete for our attention and our energy as we start our day. They flood our minds with thoughts that may cause anxiety, stress, or fear. They may not all be negative things. However, because our world is in a fallen state, we may be prone to listen to, and be drawn to, the "negative." Receiving negative information all day long can fill our emotions with negative feelings.

The world is continually sending out signals that are "up and down." Many people live their lives based upon the signals of the world, and it's like being on a roller coaster ride. If the stock market is up, they are up. If they get into an argument with their spouse, they are down. The lack of setting our focus on the Lord is prelude to living an "up and down" life. When we set our focus and fix our heart on Him, we will get an "up" signal. We will still go through difficult situations, but in Christ we can be victorious over circumstances. Jesus declared to His disciples, recorded in John 16:33, "These things I have spoken unto you, that in me ye might have peace. In the world ye shall have tribulation: but be of good cheer; I have overcome the world." Now _there's_ an up signal for the day, week, month, and year—in fact for our entire lifetime! I John 4:4 states, "Ye are of God, little children, and have overcome them: because greater is he that is in you than he that is in the world." The world will always send you "up and down" signals. If you live your life based on such signals you will vacillate emotionally, spiritually, and physically. It will seem as if you are living a "roller coaster life." Fixing our vision, affection, and concentration on God helps us to be plugged into a constant "up" signal that keeps us focused in spite of adversity.

Fix Your Heart by Praising Him!

Please note the action that David takes (Psalm 108:1-5) to fix his heart. In other words, he had to do something. Five times the word "praise," "sing," or "exalt" is used in this psalm. One of the greatest ways to set your focus and fix your heart to be steadfast and sturdy is to learn to praise Him. Praise means "to speak well of; to glorify by the attribution of perfection" (The Merriam-Webster Dictionary). In the Hebrew language, these words come together to mean "to sing, glorify, worship, to lift up your hands (a sign of surrender), to exalt and magnify."

Praise sets your focus on God's attributes. He is good. He is faithful. His mercy endures forever. He is love. He is a friend. He is kind, patient, all-wise, all-powerful, and all-knowing, to name just a few of His attributes. When we praise Him, we bring into focus His awesomeness and greatness. What will we focus on if we don't focus on the Lord? Our problems and circumstances can seem so monumental when we fail to focus on the Lord. Consider David and Goliath. David was a very young man, and Goliath was a giant and a renowned warrior! But David was focused on his God, the Lord God Jehovah, so in comparison, Goliath didn't seem unconquerable. When we rehearse our problems, verbally or just repeatedly in our mind, we magnify them. When we rehearse God's attributes, He becomes the main focus and, although the problems may still be there, they seem insignificant. Our heart is filled with hope, because God is great and He will work it all out and give us the victory! Praise is the vehicle or tool by which we can bring our heart and vision into focus on the Lord. I encourage you to let your morning prayer time be filled with praise. As you praise Him and rehearse His greatness audibly, your heart will be filled with faith, not fear, anxiety, or hopelessness.

One of the greatest ways to see how praise works in a practical sense is in a relationship between a husband and a wife. If a husband praises his wife, emphasizing and focusing on her virtues and good attributes, his attitude will be different than if he focuses on her weaknesses. I hear husbands say, "You always"...followed by a negative. Or a wife may say, "You never"... followed by a negative. In speaking in that manner, their focus is on the negative and their relationship will likely be tumultuous. However, if they start telling each other how wonderful they look or how talented they are, it will produce a very desirable result.

All human beings have faults and weakness, and at times it may require some effort for a person to see past those things in order to focus on another's strengths. However, God is absolutely perfect and has no weaknesses at all. He doesn't have an "off day." He never fails in any way. He is not surprised by any event, nor does He ever react incorrectly. We can praise Him because He is holy and He is perfect! When we do that, our attitude is dramatically affected because this great God is with us and for us!

Focus and Vision

For discussion purposes let's allow the word "vision" to describe a desire that you have in your heart to do, something that is broad in scope. Perhaps it is a passion to pursue something you feel that you were born to do. For example, you may have a vision regarding the general direction in which the Lord is leading you in your life. Vision is a "big picture" word.

Let's allow the word "focus" to refer to a narrower scope, the daily practice that propels you toward your vision. Many people have vision, but they lose their focus. They envision a grandiose idea but they lack the focus to accomplish it. If you desire to be a doctor, you must focus on the current class you are taking as a step toward accomplishing your vision. A daily focus on the Lord keeps us walking in His will.

Many people see the will of God like an impossibly thin "tightrope" stretched over a deep canyon. We feel that we have to be ever so careful not to stumble, and if we misstep, we will quickly plummet out of the purpose or plan of God. However, I believe that the will of God is more like the canyon itself, wide and deep. Walking along the floor of the canyon, if we wander too far to the right or the left, the canyon walls will effectively redirect us back toward the middle. It requires a conscious effort to climb up and out of the canyon. Likewise, as we begin to wander off the narrow path, God's love and mercy redirects us back to the center of His perfect will, and it takes a determined effort for us to climb out of His will. He is not looking to "push us off a tightrope" but rather to keep us safe and secure in the canyon of His love and grace. As we keep our focus on Him daily, He provides all we need—the strength, faith, wisdom, and guidance to fulfill His will for us.

Isaiah 40:30 teaches us that as we wait on the Lord our strength will be renewed. That indicates that if we are not waiting on the Lord, focused on Him, our strength can tend to wane. Do you often feel physically or mentally weary or exhausted? Perhaps you're not simply weary, but rather unfocused, because your precious energy has been spent and wasted on things that will not help you accomplish your vision and dream.

See the Rabbit

There is an old hunting fable of a beagle that suddenly bolted from the porch where he had been sleeping. When he took off, he began barking and causing quite a ruckus. As the beagle continued to run and bark, other neighborhood dogs became excited and began to run behind the beagle and bark as well. The lead beagle continued on into the woods, up and down hills, through thick brush and briers. One by one, the other dogs began to tire and dropped out of the race. They returned to their homes, panting and ready to collapse, but the lead beagle did not stop. He continued until he finally returned bruised and bloodied by briers. However, he had something in his mouth. It was a rabbit. The moral of the story is that the other dogs joined in the fray simply because of the noise and excitement, but the beagle persevered and won the prize because he was the only one who saw the rabbit. He was focused and his heart was fixed on getting that rabbit!

When you receive a vision and have a dream from the Lord, something that you know He desires for you to do or have, you must maintain a daily focus in order to see it come to pass. There will be many opportunities for you to drop out of the race. If you have truly "seen the rabbit" you will persevere no matter what comes your way. The focus or fixed heart comes from a heart that praises God daily. Job 9:25-26 states, "Now my days are swifter than a post: they flee away, they see no good. They are passed away as the swift ships: as the eagle that hasteth to the prey."

Pectens

In addition to a double set of eyelids, the eagle also possesses within its eyes a series of tissues called pectens. The pectens are folded into pleats. Each pleat contains a fine network of lymph tubes, and the fluid in these tubes is electrolyte. That means it is affected by magnetic pull and operates as a conductor of electricity.

An eaglet's eyes are not fully developed when it first hatches and it is unable to focus for several weeks. During this time, these tubes are pliable. They are affected by the magnetic pull of the North Pole, very similar to a compass. The pectens adjust themselves to the lines of magnetic intensity from the North Pole in relation to the eaglet's place of birth. As the eaglet matures over its first few months, the pectens become more rigid, and by the time the eaglet reaches maturity, the pectens are permanently set. As long as the eagle is away from its nesting ground there is a sense of imbalance, because the pectens are acting as a built-in gyroscope for the eagle. There is a constant pressure in the eagle's eyes which causes pain, to some degree, during times of migration. However, the pain subsides as the eagle returns to its nesting ground. It is not difficult for the eagle to find its way home even from thousands of miles away because God has equipped it with an infallible sense of direction. As the eagle approaches the nest, the pain subsides, and when the eagle is in its nest, there is absolutely no pain at all.

Are We Home Yet?

The presence and purpose of the pectens in the eagle's eyes speak volumes to us, and are a good illustration of our Christian walk. When we are young in the Lord, there is a period of time in which our spiritual eyes are developing and, of course, throughout our whole Christian life, we are constantly developing our spiritual vision. In Colossians 3:2, the Apostle Paul encouraged us to, "Set your affection on things above, not on things on the earth." The Greek word translated "set" means "to look intently." We are instructed to purposely set our affections, love, mind, and cognitive focus, on "things above." It is sometimes challenging to keep in mind that ultimate success is not achieved here on earth, but rather it is finally achieved in our spiritual home in eternity with the Lord. Heaven is our "nest" and there is a "pull" in our hearts toward that destination!

As born again believers, our ultimate "home" for eternity is heaven, where we will dwell in the presence of the Lord with all believers. We can be comforted by the fact that we are heading to that destination when our life on earth is done. However, while we are alive here on earth, we can experience a wonderful "home away from home" that is as close as we can get to heaven on earth. That place is called the presence of the Lord.

As a young believer, like the eaglet, it takes time for us to develop spiritual, heavenly eyesight. Some people live a lifetime on earth and never really see beyond the present. They never live beyond the rat race and the endless cycle of "I have to go to work to make the money to buy the bread to get the strength...

to go to work to make the money to buy the bread to get the strength…and on and on." It is not that things like work, money, and food are wrong or unnecessary. It is just that these things are temporary. Our long term vision should be set on what we will have in heaven.

In the movie "Gladiator," the Roman General Maximus delivered a stirring speech to his soldiers just prior to battle. He declared, "What we do in life echoes in eternity." There is truth in that statement. What will *you* do today that will echo in eternity? What will you do today that will have value after today and tomorrow, or thirty, forty, or fifty years from now? How we live for the Lord on earth echoes in eternity. Our Christian witness affects the lives of others, which in turn echoes in eternity. For example, how we treat our spouses and children, and how we conduct ourselves in our workplace and community, produces an echo in eternity.

Setting Our Sights On Things Above: Like the Eagle, Not the Chicken!

We must take time to develop eyesight for what God describes as "things above." He defines "things above" by presenting its antithesis, "not on things on the earth." (Colossians 3:2) Chickens spend most of their lives with their heads down. They peck in the ground for their food. Chickens really don't fly, and they certainly don't soar. I am glad that Isaiah didn't write that our strength will be renewed and we will soar like chickens! Please note that the title of this book is not, "Like the Chicken." Now, I have absolutely nothing against chickens. However, the eagle soars in the skies and has a vision of the heavens that a chicken can only dream about. Like a chicken, many people set their sights on things that will soon fade away and vanish, things that are temporal. Some of them have already vanished. We must learn, like the eagle, to set our sights on things above. Be like the eagle, not like the chicken!

Have you ever experienced a big disappointment as a result of setting your affections on something that was temporal? Miriam Webster's Dictionary defines temporal as "of or relating to time as opposed to eternity; of or relating to earthly life; lay or secular rather than clerical or sacred." People are disappointed, sometimes even crushed, every day by things that are temporal, things that relate to the earthly life only. It does not mean that these are necessarily sinful things. It just means that these things do not have an eternal quality to them. We must get our eyes focused on eternal things rather than temporal things.

Empty and Unfulfilled

Our world today is full of temporal things that do not satisfy. Perhaps this point is made most profoundly by Solomon writing in Chapter 2 of Ecclesiastes. Solomon pursued many earthly pleasures to determine whether his deepest longings could be fulfilled by things on earth. He performed great works, built houses, experienced laughter, planted gardens and orchards, and made pools of water (swimming pools). He had many servants and many "maidens" (women). He acquired cattle (possessions), and he also had much silver and gold (money).

In modern vernacular, we could say Solomon "hit it big." He achieved the American Dream of success. He had a huge mansion like the ones we see in magazines or on television, complete with swimming pool and hot tub. What a life! He had many parties and a "posse" who followed him around. He owned large tracts of land on which to ride horses, and beautiful gardens to find solace for his soul. He owned a big company with many employees that obeyed his commands. He enjoyed the companionship of many beautiful women. He experienced a couple of great years in the stock market and made so much money he didn't know how to spend it all. Many people would call a person in this situation blessed and prosperous. However, we learn from Scripture that something significant was missing in Solomon's life.

Ecclesiastes 2:10 tells us that Solomon had his eyes upon these earthly things. His focus was on pleasure rather than God. When our eyes are on these types of things, we will likely feel as Solomon did, when he effectively wrote, "Something is missing. I am left empty and unfulfilled." Ecclesiastes 2:10-11 states, "And whatsoever mine eyes desired I kept not from them; I withheld not my heart from any joy; for my heart rejoiced because of all my labor; and this was my portion from all my labor. Then I looked on all the works that my hands had wrought, and on the labor that I had labored to do; and, behold, all was vanity and a striving after wind, and there was no profit under the sun."

The Hebrew word translated "vanity" means "emptiness; something transitory and unsatisfactory; often used as an adverb: altogether vain." The Hebrew word translated "vexation" or "striving after wind" means "to grasp." Solomon came to the conclusion that when he set his eyes on these things, he was empty and unfulfilled. How can that be?

Longing For Home

I believe that the answer is found in the great wisdom that Solomon communicates through his writings later in that same book. Ecclesiastes 3:11 declares "He <God> hath made everything beautiful in its time: also he hath set eternity in their heart, yet so that man cannot find out the work that God hath done from the beginning even to the end." The moment we are born again, we become aware that there is a place called home that we have not yet seen. Heaven is our eternal home. Like the eagle, God has built into our spiritual vision a place called home. The further we get from that place, the more pain and emptiness we find. When we set our eyes upon our eternal "nest" (heaven), we can find a place of peace and rest. We have an internal spiritual gyroscope that knows we are not in the place God has designed us to be forever. We are passing through. There is an eternal longing for home!

Home Away From Home

Psalm 16:11 declares, "Thou wilt shew me the path of life: In thy presence is fulness of joy; at thy right hand there are pleasures for evermore." God bids us in Psalm 100:2-4, "Serve the Lord with gladness: Come before his presence with singing. Know ye that the Lord he is God: It is he that hath made us, and not we ourselves; we are his people, and the sheep of his pasture. Enter into his gates with thanksgiving, and into his courts with praise: be thankful unto him, and bless his name."

These verses give us great comfort in the fact that, though we are not currently in heaven, we have access to God's presence in this life to satisfy our longing soul. We can have a taste of eternal joy here on earth—not through physical, earthly, temporal things, but by spending time with Him and abiding in His presence. The presence of God is essentially our "home away from home" here on the earth. How do we avoid the pitfalls of being trapped in a temporal life that will equate to vanity? No one wants to be unsatisfied, unfulfilled, and chasing a life of meaningless possessions. Please note that I am not saying that God does not want us to work hard and be diligent in our labor. In fact, Proverbs 21:5 states, "The plans of the diligent lead surely to advantage." (NASB) But in all of our pursuing, we must not forget that the most important pursuit is God, and being in His presence. That is what brings true fulfillment. His presence is our "home away from home."

John wrote, as recorded in John 15:4, the powerful yet simple words of Jesus, "Abide in me, and I in you." God wants us to set our eyes upon Him and eternal things. We understand that temporal things are not evil in and of themselves. God wants us to be blessed here on the earth, but to also always be mindful that possessions and achievements without His presence can only bring temporal fulfillment, and they will not satisfy the deep longing for home. A great hymn entitled "Near to the Heart of God" communicates this truth. The lyrics declare, "There is a place of quiet rest, near to the heart of God, a place where sin cannot molest, near to the heart of God." [1]

Good to Be Near God

In Psalm 73, Asaph writes of the perplexity of the riches of the wicked. To him, it appeared as though the wicked were having a great party all the time and were prosperous and happy. It appeared as though they had no cares or troubles, even though they did not honor God. When Asaph observed this (and it is likely that all of us have had similar experiences), he effectively stated that it was very hard for him to understand. Asaph writes in Psalm 73:16-17, "When I thought I might know this, It was too painful for me; Until I went into the sanctuary of God and considered their latter end." (ASV)

The sanctuary of God is symbolic of His presence. Their "latter end" was never finding home, but only enjoying the temporary party and temporal things. The last verse is so simple if we can just grasp it. Like the eagle, we know where home is; we know where the nest is. It is in the presence of God. While here on earth, the nest is being in communion with Him, until we reach heaven where we will never leave His presence. Like the eagle, until we get to the nest there will be some painful experiences. Asaph discerned a great theological truth that is so simple and so obvious, yet many miss it. He ultimately came to a profound conclusion which is recorded in Psalm 73:28, "But it is good for me to draw near to God: I have put my trust in the Lord GOD, that I may declare all thy works." Regardless of how things look, and who seems to be prospering around us, all that matters is that it is good for us to be near God!

You Can Always Find Your Way Home

Many people find themselves wandering away from the nest of God's presence. Perhaps it is because of sin, obsessive business ambitions, lust for pleasures or possessions, or simply the stresses and pressures of life. Many times, difficult circumstances bring great pain into people's lives, making it seem like they cannot find rest for their soul. Many people are filled with anxiety, longing, frustration, loneliness, and emptiness. They have become lost in life and have somehow lost their way, struggling to deal with the pain in their heart. The great news is that we have within us the roadmap to get home. It is the Holy Spirit within us that is drawing us back to His presence. His presence is like the nest to the eagle. The closer we get to God, the more the pain subsides, even as the pain in the eagle's eyes subsides as he nears his nest, which is his home.

Isaiah 53:6 declares that "All we like sheep have gone astray; we have turned every one to his own way." God knows that our fallen flesh is prone to wander away and, like Solomon, we sometimes try to chase the winds of success, money, power, and earthly possessions. That is why God put within us an internal gyroscope, a compass to get us home. In the parable of the prodigal son in Luke Chapter 15, the son took his riches and went far from home, but when he had spent all of the money, he had one desire in his heart. He wanted desperately to go home. When he finally arrived home, he found the most beautiful thing. His father was waiting for him and came running to meet him, warmly welcoming him home, and desiring to meet all of his needs.

God built within the eagle's eyes not only the ability to see where it is, but the ability to see and know where it was not. Have you ever been on a trip and looked up and noticed that nothing looked familiar? We now have GPS (Global Positioning System) technology. Via satellite communication, a GPS unit can show us where we are, where we want to be, and how to find our way there. We also have a GPS in our spirit that can help us find our way to His presence, His voice, His comfort, His Healing, and most importantly His fulfillment "...in His presence is the fullness of joy..." (Psalm 16:11)

When you are feeling empty, follow the compass, the GPS unit, of your spirit. Come home. Get back to the nest of God's presence. Begin to talk with Him and worship Him. Pick up the Bible, the living Word of God. Study it and let it be absorbed into your longing heart, and the pain will subside. You will realize, as did Asaph in Psalm 73:28, "It is good for me to be near God."

My Personal Testimony

After working in the secular business world for about eighteen years, I was attempting to juggle my work responsibilities and pastor a small church that I had planted. There were many challenging things that occurred as I attempted to balance both worlds. I knew, however, that the Lord had spoken to me about leaving my position in the secular world to go into fulltime ministry. As I was praying about this decision, many of my colleagues in the business world thought I had lost my mind because I had experienced what many would consider outstanding success. They would say, "This is what you should be doing, you will be back."

However, I knew that God was guiding me to pastor full time. It was perhaps one of the biggest decisions I have faced in my life. I had tremendous security in the business world in contrast to a relatively small church in the ministry. Nevertheless, I knew the direction to which God was calling me, and I ultimately obeyed His voice. I wish I could say it was an easy road, but it was not. There were some difficult times when God sent people to help us financially so we could meet our needs. I could not see the total "vision" that God had for me as I endeavored to lead that small church and touch the community with the gospel of Jesus Christ. I had no idea that it would mean overseeing seven building programs to keep up with the growing number of people that God was sending who needed healing and restoration.

I had a vision to minister restoration to hurting people. I just didn't know entirely what that would entail. We started a church with five people (all family members), and ultimately, before I retired from the fulltime pastorate, the Lord had enabled us to build a 3,000 seat sanctuary. After 48 years of pastoring the same church, I could see what God had intended. Through all the high times and hard times, disappointments and victories, all I really knew was that God had put a "vision" in my heart to love and help people that had been broken and hurting, to minister life and wholeness to them. He put a "theme" scripture on my heart, Zechariah 4:6, which declares, "...Not by might, nor by power, but by my spirit, saith the LORD of hosts." It seemed at times that God's leading defied human logic. However, I had a vision and I endeavored, to the best of my ability, to follow that vision. It unfolded in unexpected ways and through various miracles. Looking back, I believe that if I had stayed in the business world, I never would have completed God's assignment for my life.

This is why it is so critical to develop that spiritual eye-sight—to keep our focus directly on the Son! Whenever I felt like I was getting off track, or I was apprehensive about the next step, I would go back and rehearse the vision and lean upon those words in Zechariah 4:6. If it was going to be done, it had to be done by the power of the Holy Spirit. Keeping a focused vision can be difficult in the face of problems we encounter in life, but God had put a "gyroscope" within me, a way to find my direction. It is by His Spirit and by being obedient to His voice.

Whenever we find ourselves feeling that we are lost, we can return to the place of God's presence and hear His reassuring voice. If your relationship is not where it should be, come home. If you have pain in your life, you can come home to His presence and be held in His arms and He can heal the pain. If you feel lonely and lost, remember that He is the way, the truth, and the life (John 14:6). Get close to Him. If you struggle with anger and unforgiveness, He can give you the strength to forgive. That pain and discomfort you are feeling is the God-made "gyroscope" in your spirit telling you to get closer to Him! We know that God has promised never to leave us nor forsake us (Hebrews 13:5), but at times we wander from His path. Thank God for the example of the eagle that shows us how God puts the ability inside us to find our way home.

Will you join me in this prayer right now? "God, I want to be close to You and walk with You. I am sorry I have allowed distractions to separate me from You. Forgive me for my sin. Cleanse me today (I John 1:9). Give me a new start. Lord, and heal any pain in me that is keeping me from You. Help me to trust You with all the areas of my life. Give me strength to forgive those that have hurt me, and please help those whom I have hurt to forgive me. I love You Lord, and I thank You that You will never leave me nor forsake me. Help me not to leave You, and keep me in the center of Your will. Amen."

CHAPTER 2

Like the Eagle in Reproduction and Maturation

The Bible does not give us great detail about the early life of Jesus, but one scripture that does speak volumes to us is Luke 2:52, which states, "And Jesus grew in wisdom, and stature, and in favor with God and man." Even Jesus, who was God incarnate, had to learn to grow in wisdom and knowledge. Every believer is constantly in a growing process. We must become comfortable with this process! No one knows everything, and our knowledge here on earth will never be complete until we meet the Lord face to face one day. We need not be ashamed of what we do not know. Conversely, we should not be proud of what we do know, because God is always teaching us something, and there is always much more to be learned.

Building a Nest

We can learn some fundamental lessons from how the eagle builds his nest as two eagles prepare to have eaglets.

First, the eagle begins to look for a location that is best for its nest. In business, some say "location is everything," and the goal is to identify a location that many people will be able to see and access. The eagle's thinking is different, however, because it looks for a spot that is hidden. Some eagle nests are as high as 10,000 feet and in a rock cleft, unseen by the human eye from the ground. The average eagle will spend approximately 50 years in this nest so finding the best location is of the utmost importance. This is home! They look for a spot that is permanent. It is to be a place that affords safety and comfort, and a place to teach their eaglets to become mature eagles. They look for a place to build a nest which is on a rock and where their back is against a rock wall. Psalm 18:1-2 declares, "I love Thee, O Lord, my strength. The Lord is my rock and my fortress and my deliverer. My God, my rock in whom I take refuge; My shield and the horn of my salvation, my stronghold."

A rock is a solid place. A number of years ago, I had the opportunity to drive through mountains on the west coast of the Unites States. These mountains have been there for many years through storms, tornadoes, rains, fires, and floods. God is much like this. When His Word declares Him as a rock, it is referring to a mountain, a huge mass, an immovable object. What better place to build a foundation?

As you fall in love with the Lord and begin to grow in His Word and in relationship with Him, you are in effect building a nest. Psalm 91 speaks of the secret place where the Lord hides us. You can dwell in His presence and be safe. It is a place in which you can live. I believe that every time we pray we are returning to that "nest" of His presence! Job 39:27-29 states, "Does the eagle mount up...and make his nest on high? On the cliff he dwells....upon the point of the rock."

It is important to note that eagles take weeks to build their nest. They make hundreds of flights to the ground to find branches that can hold the weight of their nest—a nest that will eventually weigh hundreds of pounds. Many times they carry materials that are heavier than their own body to build a place where they and their future family can be safe.

Building a Foundation

Another lesson that we can learn from the eagle is about building a foundation. Luke 6:47-48 declares, "Whosoever cometh to me, and heareth my sayings, and doeth them, I will shew you to whom he is like: He is like a man which built an house, and digged deep, and laid the foundation on a rock: and when the flood arose, the stream beat vehemently upon that house, and could not shake it: for it was founded upon a rock."

The foundation of a building is its base, a supportive structure that holds up the building. A strong foundation can lead to a strong building, but a weak foundation will ultimately be revealed, no matter how good the superstructure appears. Foundations in the Lord begin with knowing the work He has done for you on the cross. Following are some foundational truths upon which to build your life.

1. *God chose you*. Ephesians 1:3-4 states, "Blessed be the God and Father or our Lord Jesus Christ who has blessed us with every spiritual blessing in the heavenly places in Christ, just as He chose us in Him before the foundation of the world, that we would he holy and blameless before Him..." (NASB)

2. *God saved you*. Ephesians 2:8-9 declares, "For by grace are ye saved through faith; and that not of yourselves: it is the gift of God: Not of works, lest any man should boast."

3. *God has made you His child*. I John 3:3 states, "Beloved, now we are children of God." (NASB)

4. *God has called you to a purpose in life*. II Timothy 1:9 declares, "...who has saved us, and called us with a holy calling, not according to our works, but according to His own purpose and grace which was granted us in Christ Jesus from all eternity." (NASB)

5. <u>*God has a plan for you to mature spiritually.*</u> II Peter 3:18 states, "but grow in the grace and knowledge of our Lord and Savior Jesus Christ." (NASB)

Our foundation begins with knowing that we were chosen by God. His desire is for everyone to choose Him. Many do not, but that is their choice alone. God saved us, which means He cleansed us from every sin that would or could keep us from relationship and eternity with Him. He has made us a part of His family. He is our Father and we are His children. God has also set in motion a purpose for each and every life, a plan in which He wants to use us to share the Gospel and further His kingdom. He also has a plan for us to mature. Just as a baby grows by eating and receiving nurturing, we mature in Christ as we study His Word, pray, and fellowship with His family.

As we walk with God, circumstances may arise that threaten to "shake" our foundation. I have met many people that feel like God is distant or that He has forgotten them. Of course, that is not the case. We have a foundation in Him that cannot be changed, moved, shaken, or displaced. Luke 6:46-49 not only teaches us the importance of building our foundation on the "rock," who is Christ, but is a reminder that we have such a foundation that cannot be moved. Even when we go through shaky times and uncertain events, He is immutable. Therefore, the eternal truths that secure our salvation and relationship with Him cannot change!

The eagle will make hundreds of trips to gather material that is on the ground with which to build its nest. What determination! In today's world we want things quickly. We want things overnight. We want to go to church like a fast food drive-thru and get the material we need in one hour with which to build our lives. That kind of thinking is deceptive. God has given us the "building materials" of His Word, fellowship with other believers, and most importantly fellowship with Him. Don't grow weary if you feel like you are not getting anywhere. It requires many trips to the Word, to the altar, to your quiet place with the Lord, but each time you build a stronger foundation, a stronger nest for your life, family, and business. You might not see the results of your efforts overnight, but be persistent. If you have not started, start today. Start with prayer and studying the Word. John Chapter 15 is a good place to begin. Start learning, start growing, and by all means, *start today*! You will build a foundation that will stand the test of any storm in life.

Inspect the Foundation

During my pastoral ministry, I counseled many people that were going through a crisis of some kind. Many times these individuals felt lost, confused, and desperate for answers. In talking with them, I would examine their foundation. Like a structural engineer who looks at the foundation of a building, I would look at the foundation of their life. I would do so by asking questions about the amount of time they spent regularly in personal devotions, Bible study, and prayer, as well as how faithful they were in church attendance. Often, they were sorely lacking in these fundamental areas, and therefore their spiritual foundation was very weak. You see, if we don't spend time building our spiritual foundation, we will feel as lost and hurting as the victims of natural disasters when crisis comes to our life. We will feel like the floods and the winds have taken everything away from us. The difficult situations and problems we encounter in life are real, but there is nothing like having a foundation that can't be moved, a place to which we can return to obtain peace, rest, and wisdom for the future.

Growing Pains

The father and mother eagle work hard to prepare a place for their eaglets. Shortly before the eaglet is born, the mother eagle begins to pull feathers from her breast and lay them upon the sticks on the bottom of the nest. This serves to comfort the young eaglets as they are birthed. They are born into a soft, fluffy, down floor made from the mother eagle's feathers. Not only do these feathers provide comfort and warmth, but they also carry the scent of the mother. When she is away from the nest, the eaglets are comforted by her scent on the feathers, and they understand that "mom" is not far away.

When we are young believers we experience much of this same treatment. We are born again into the loving arms and soft, forgiving grace of the Lord. We find a place of rest from our works and sins of the flesh. We find a nest of unconditional love. We don't need to perform for it, earn it, or do anything to deserve it. As a matter of fact, we can't do any of the above. We can only say "yes" to Him, be born of His Spirit, and rest in the warmth of His love. We are even fed directly from the provision that the Father has secured for us. We can eat of the spoils of Jesus' victory on the cross. We can partake of love, joy, kindness, forgiveness, healing, restoration, and peace! He has brought these things to the nest of salvation in the rock of His protection. What a place to be born!

The eaglet continues in this environment for a considerable time as it begins to grow and mature. However, eventually and inevitably, there comes a day when the mother eagle comes home and begins to stir the nest and cause a commotion. She begins to stomp around the nest and, using her wings and beak, she begins to clear out all the feathers that the eaglets have been comfortably lying on. She begins to "clean house." The mother eagle kicks out all of the feathers so that the sticks begin to poke the eaglets and they are forced to stand up on their talons. This may seem cruel, but it is the beginning of the stirring of the nest as referred to in Deuteronomy 32:11, which states, "like an eagle that stirs up its nest and hovers over its young." (NIV) The mother eagle is causing the eaglets to begin to strengthen their legs and sharpen their talons which will equip them to lay hold of a rabbit one day. The mother eagle is preparing the eaglet for its future.

Strengthened!

The Bible speaks about strengthening in a number of scriptures. Recorded in Luke 22:31-32, Jesus said, "Simon, Simon, behold, Satan has demanded permission to sift you like wheat; but I have prayed for you, that your faith may not fail; and you, when once you have turned again, strengthen your brothers." (NASB) I Corinthians 15:13 declares, "Be on the alert, stand firm in the faith, act like men, be strong." (NASB) 2 Thessalonians 2:16-17 states, "Now may our Lord Jesus Christ Himself and God our Father, who has loved us and given us eternal comfort and good hope by grace, comfort and strengthen your hearts in every good work and word." (NASB) Romans 4:20 refers to Abraham when it declares, "Yet with respect to the promise of God, he did not waiver in unbelief but grew strong in faith, giving glory to God." (NASB)

God wants us to understand this principle of strengthening. We must learn that walking with God is a constant growth and maturation process. Jesus told Peter that when he had been strengthened, then he would strengthen others. Abraham was strengthened in his faith. Paul told the men in the church at Corinth to "be strong." At times we may think that God or his Word seems harsh, but that is not true. _God is trying to prepare us for a world system that is not going to give us a comforter made of soft feathers._ If we make up our mind to live for God, we will need to grow and become strong! The good news is that God will strengthen us every step of the way. It is His Spirit that makes us strong. Philippians 4:13 declares that we can do all things through Christ who strengthens us!

We all likely have a warm image in our mind of Jesus with loving arms. He certainly is that and so much more. However, at times and seasons in our life, He is also the mother eagle that comes and stirs the nest and says, "It is time to get those legs strong and talons sharp. I am going to teach you how to be victorious."

Whenever we are moving from one plateau to the next in life, we must be aware that this strengthening process will take place. Perhaps we are moving from a job or ministry in which we have been comfortable. I have known church members who became offended if someone else sat in "their" Sunday morning pew. God says, "Get ready, because it is time to be strengthened. Get ready to move."

In life, a time of strengthening almost always precedes a time of transition to a new place or a new segment of the journey. You may feel that God is being cruel, or your boss or pastor is being harsh. However, it may be a time of strengthening in which the feathers of your nest are being kicked out from under you, and you must learn to stand up. It may not be comfortable, but you must keep in mind that you are being equipped for the future. The little eaglets were not aware that their talons, which were being sharpened by the sticks, would soon be lethal weapons capable of stabbing their prey in flight. The eaglets were not happy at the time of the strengthening, but they were glad later when they had acquired the tools to get the job done! Their talons had become sharp enough to hold onto the prey they had grasped. Many people have not been prepared to hold on to the success which they have attained. God may be strengthening you so that you will have the faith to hold on to that which God has given you!

Flying Lessons

The lessons for the eaglet in the nest have only begun. Soon after the eaglet begins to be strengthened, and is able to stand, and its talons are sharper, the mother returns again with more seemingly cold and indifferent behavior. This time the lesson is taught in tandem. The father eagle flies above the nest while the mother eagle begins lesson number two. The mother again begins to stir the nest by flapping her wings wildly. Instead of sitting on the edge of the nest, which is her normal perch, she begins to violently move around inside the nest until the eaglet is forced to the edge. The eaglet now is facing a terrifying moment. Surely the eaglet is thinking that the mother eagle is trying to kill it because this time her fluttering actually forces the eaglet over the side and out of the nest. Be reminded that these nests can be as high as 10,000 feet in the air! The eaglet suddenly finds itself plummeting toward certain death.

A phenomenon occurs at this point. The survival instinct rises up in the eaglet and it begins flapping its wings with all the frantic strength it can muster. Most often the eaglet continues this until it is just a few thousand feet from the ground. At this desperate point, the father eagle begins his role in the lesson. The father eagle goes into a dive position and targets the small eaglet, catching it just before the point of no return. The father eagle returns the eaglet to the nest for a rest and then the process begins again. All of the test flights are initiated by the mother eagle and terminated by the father eagle. The parents are waiting for the moment when the eaglet fully imitates its parents by stretching out its wings and catching the updraft of the wind.

After a few more test flights, the eaglet understands, relaxes, and catches the updraft. It soon realizes that flying is quite effortless if it lets the wind do most of the work. Throughout the learning process, regardless of how many times the eaglet is plummeting toward earth with no idea of how to save itself, the father eagle is faithful to swoop down, rescue the eaglet, and return it to the nest. The father eagle will do this faithfully until the lesson is learned. Likewise, our loving Father is patient with us and He is ever faithful to rescue us as we are learning to "fly" as a Christian.

Isaiah 40:30-31 declares, "Even the youths shall faint and be weary, and the young men shall utterly fall: But they that wait upon the LORD shall renew their strength; they shall mount up with wings as eagles; they shall run, and not be weary; and they shall walk, and not faint." John 3:8 states, "The wind blows where it wishes and you hear the sound of it, but do not know where it comes from and where it is going; so is everyone who is born of the Spirit." (NASB) Galatians 5:16 declares, "Walk by the Spirit, and you will not carry out the desire of the flesh." (NASB) Romans 8:26 states, "And in the same way the Spirit also helps our weakness; for we do not know how to pray as we should, but the Spirit Himself intercedes for us with groanings too deep for words." (NASB)

Romans 8:9b, 11 declares, "...if indeed the Spirit of God dwells in you. But if anyone does not have the Spirit of Christ, he does not belong to Him...But if the Spirit of Him who raised Jesus from the dead dwells in you, He who raised Christ Jesus from the dead will also give life to your mortal bodies through His Spirit who dwells in you." (NASB) The Spirit of God comes to live inside of us when we receive Christ. He is symbolized by the wind in the Bible and He is as important to the believer as the wind is to the eagle. As the eagle needs the wind to soar into the sky, we need the Spirit to soar above adversity in life. Paul encouraged the Ephesians (Ephesians 5:18), "Do not get drunk on wine…Instead, be filled with the Spirit." (NIV) He was commanding and instructing us to be filled with God and everything that He is.

God wants us to walk in a relationship with His Holy Spirit. We are filled with the Spirit as we spend time with God. He abides in us (John 14:17). Putting it simply, we can ask God to fill us with His Holy Spirit, and He will. We can ask the Holy Spirit to "help" us in our everyday life, and He will, according to Romans 8:26 and John 16:7. The Holy Spirit is our peace (John 14:27). He will give us strength (Romans 8:11). He convicts us of sin and wrong (John 16:8). The Holy Spirit is our teacher (John 14:26) and He will guide us at all times (John 16:13). John 14:16 also says that He will be with us forever! These are awesome and empowering truths. The Holy Spirit is with us, in us, and He will never leave us!

The Spotter

In a weightlifting exercise known as a bench press, a weightlifter lies on a weight bench, lifts the weight off the supporting bars, lowers it to his chest, and then lifts ("presses") it back up. It may seem easy at first, but lifting even the lightest weight repeatedly can cause his arms to weaken and even shake. Eventually, he will find it difficult to lift the weight. Thankfully, for him, there is a person nearby who is referred to as the "spotter." The spotter stands near the weightlifter's head, and his responsibility is to help the weightlifter lift the weight when he gets tired. If there is no spotter present, and the weightlifter tries to lift too much weight, the weight will crash down on his chest and he could be seriously injured. No experienced weightlifter attempts to bench press without a spotter.

Similarly, the pressures of life often seem too great for us to bear. At times, things may seem easy, but at other times they may seem to be too heavy to carry. Temptation, loneliness, financial pressures, and poor health are examples. We may feel that we are going to be crushed under their weight. I have good news for you, though—you have a spotter that never leaves you nor forsakes you. The Holy Spirit is there to help you in the "press" of life. Jesus said, "In this world, you will have tribulation, but take heart because I have overcome the world." (John 16:33) The Greek word translated "tribulation" is *thlipsis,* which means pressure and stress.

You can try to "fly" without the Holy Spirit, but if you try to rely upon your human knowledge, business sense, and ingenuity, inevitably you will find yourself like the eaglet, profusely beating its wings, but yet still plummeting toward the ground. I am so thankful that when we are learning to fly and we begin to fall, the **Holy** Spirit, just like the father eagle, swoops down, picks us **up, and** brings us back to the nest of safety and love. As in the **popular** song "Wind Beneath My Wings,"[2] the Holy Spirit is **always there** to catch us and carry us to safety. He is the true wind **beneath** our wings. He is our strength. He is always there. Simply **talk** to Him, all the time, and ask Him for help in everything you do. You will soon be soaring to new heights in the power of the Spirit. You can frantically flap your wings, pant, and struggle, or you can listen for, and respond to, the Holy Spirit. The words of the prophet Zechariah (4:6) declare, "Not by might, nor my power, but by my Spirit saith the Lord of Hosts."

CHAPTER 3

Like the Eagle in Diet

"You are what you eat" is a phrase that is often used concerning diet. The phrase infers that your diet affects your strength, health, attitude and outlook on life. This principle holds true with the eagle as well. One of the big reasons the eagle is such a mighty creature is because of what the eagle eats.

The Eagle's Selective Diet

The eagle is often described as a "finicky" eater by those who study it. The eagle is extremely selective and requires a certain diet, and it will not compromise that diet for any reason. While other birds are willing to eat berries, insects, and carcasses of dead animals, this is not true of the eagle. The eagle chooses its diet every day. The eagle may choose fish one day, squirrel another, and possibly lamb or rabbit on another. It seemingly knows the nutritional value of each animal and it selects a specific one for each day. The eagle does not eat what it finds; it finds what it needs!

The eagle has incredible hunting skills because of its vision, its ability to dive at speeds approaching 200 miles per hour, and its ability to seize its prey with its sharp talons. Eagles have been seen flying at 10,000 feet, carrying animals that are heavier than their own body weight. The eagle first decides or discerns what it wants to eat, flying high above the earth until it finds it, dives down and latches onto it with its talons, and carries it back to its nest while the prey is still warm. The eagle will have very little, if anything at all, to do with decomposed meat.

We can see many spiritual parallels relating to how we resemble the eagle in diet. We are what we eat, so we need to ask ourselves, in a spiritual sense, "How has my diet been?" Our spiritual diet can be defined by the things that we ingest, absorb, and allow into our hearts and minds. The things that we read, watch, listen to, and meditate upon can be considered the elements of our spiritual diet. Many Christians live their whole lives indiscriminately "eating" whatever is convenient or whatever is available on the path of least resistance. I fear that living in today's world, we have become less selective, despite the fact that God has created and instructed us to be very selective. We replace prayer with Christian television. We choose churches based on the length of the service, the beauty of the facilities, or the economic status of the congregation. What about the spiritual food that is being served? Are we getting the spiritual nourishment that we need?

I am reminded of the time when Jesus told His listeners (John Chapter 6) that they must eat of His flesh and drink of His blood. Jesus wasn't referring to ingesting His physical flesh and blood. Rather, He was exhorting His listeners to identify with His death and the price He would pay for the forgiveness of our sins. The Bible says that many of His followers left Him because the things Jesus was saying were too hard for them. He asked the twelve if they were going to leave also. He declared to them (John 6:63) "It is the spirit that quickeneth; the flesh profiteth nothing: the words that I speak unto you, they are spirit, and they are life." Peter responded, knowing Jesus spoke God's word, which was the food Peter wanted and needed. Peter was determined not to leave Jesus. John 6:68 states, "Then Simon Peter answered him, 'Lord, to whom shall we go? Thou hast the words of eternal life.'"

Fast Food Spirituality

In teaching the disciples how they should pray, Jesus said, "Give us this day our daily bread." (Matthew 6:11) We need a daily word from the Lord. The Word of God is like food to our spirit man. It feeds us and keeps us strong and healthy. I encourage you to "find your word." Peter was a man that found his word; he found life in the words that came from Jesus. It is easy to obtain a fast food meal in a drive-thru restaurant, but a steady diet of that kind of food will eventually be detrimental to our health. I am concerned that we may be living in a "fast food" spiritual society. Some people go to church and frequently look at their watch, anxiously anticipating the conclusion of the service. Others simply read the Bible out of habit or routine. It is good to practice that routine, but it is better to search for the specific word that the Lord desires to speak to us for each particular day.

We are responsible as believers to search the Word of God for our own life and our own walk with the Lord. It is not the pastor's responsibility, nor the responsibility of anyone else. There are answers in the Word of God. We can find whatever we need in the Bible. When facing financial difficulties, we can study the Bible and find the plan that God has for our finances. When facing physical illness, we need to read I Peter 2:24, which declares that we are healed because of the "stripes" that Jesus took on His back, shedding His blood as the Romans whipped him mercilessly. Like the eagle, we have to selectively and aggressively "go after" our food.

Psalm 1:2 refers to a believer when it declares, "But his delight is in the law of the LORD; and in his law doth he meditate day and night." We are admonished and encouraged to do more than just read the Bible; we are to study and meditate on it. The Hebrew word translated "meditate" means "to ponder in a studious manner." Like the eagle, we can sink our "talons" of faith into the Word and it becomes "our word." God has a specific word that is in season for each day, month, year, and situation! It is our responsibility to seek out that specific word. Proverbs 25:2 states, "It is the glory of God to conceal a thing: but the honour of kings is to search out a matter." Luke 11:9 declares, "And I say unto you, Ask, and it shall be given you; seek, and ye shall find; knock, and it shall be opened unto you." Every believer is responsible to ask, seek, and knock when approaching the Word of God.

Perhaps you have fallen into the trap of just eating whatever you "find." If so, I encourage you to begin to ask specifically for the Lord to speak to you through His Word. It is your spiritual food. It is "life" as Peter declared in John 6:68. Picture a body builder on the outside and a weak, puny little man on the inside. This is the state of many believers who do not seek, study, and meditate on the Word of God. There are no shortcuts to our spiritual growth; it comes from the Word of God.

Eagles or Vultures?

Please note that the eagle eats only "live" prey. It does not concern itself with things that are dead. The eagle does not waste time, energy and effort on something that will not bring nourishment. It wants something fresh and nutritious. The eagle has a cousin in the bird family called the vulture. The vulture's diet and lifestyle is opposite the eagle's. The vulture builds its nest in dead trees or on the ground. Its head and neck are featherless so it can more readily stick its head into a dead carcass without the carcass sticking to it. The diet of the vulture is a diet of leftovers. There is nothing selective about the diet of the vulture. It will feed on a dead carcass until it becomes so bloated that it is unable to fly, and in that condition, it can become prey itself. Feeding upon the "dead things" of this world will prevent us from being able to function the way the Lord has created us to function. The diet of the vulture renders it weak and helpless, and puts it in the position of becoming prey.

The diet of the vulture is like the diet of our culture! In other words, the vulture has a diet that is chosen by the circumstances and events of life and death. It eats what it finds. It eats what is dead! This world has a lot of dead things to offer. Hollywood produces dynamic and glitzy productions, but most of them do not bring life to our spirit. We watch too much television, "flying" through the remote control hour after hour, and much of which we are consuming during this channel-surfing only brings death. Many people spend much time gossiping, which is like feeding on a dead carcass. Tragically, millions are caught in the trap of pornography, wasting countless hours and dollars, and in the end it brings only death to their minds, marriages, and ability to hear from God. Let's not be a "culture of vultures" but rather an army of eagles!

The World or the Word

Numbers 11:4-6 states, "And the mixed multitude that was among them fell a lusting: and the children of Israel also wept again, and said, Who shall give us flesh to eat? We remember the fish, which we did eat in Egypt freely; the cucumbers, and the melons, and the leeks, and the onions, and the garlick: But now our soul is dried away: there is nothing at all, beside this manna, before our eyes."

The children of Israel had a diet problem. They had become accustomed to the food of Egypt, which is symbolic of the "world" and its systems. They were complaining about the manna that God had provided for their provision. Once you develop an appetite for the "world," it is difficult to break. The only thing that will destroy an appetite for the world is time in the Word of God.

John 8:31-32 declares, "Then said Jesus to those Jews which believed on him, If ye continue in my word, then are ye my disciples indeed; And ye shall know the truth, and the truth shall make you free." The Word of God is truth and it is our spiritual food. If we have an appetite that we know we need to break, looking into the Word of God will make us free. It does not always happen overnight, and that is why Jesus used the word "make," which refers to a process. That is also why verse 31 encourages us to "continue" in the Word! It is not just a one time experience, but rather a daily walk in the Word of God, seeking Jesus, who liberates us through every word that we read, meditate upon, and apply to our lives.

Who Chooses Your Diet?

The question you must ask yourself is "Who chooses my diet?" Within every person, there is an ongoing battle between the appetites of the flesh and those of the spirit, and the winner of that battle chooses the diet. Who chooses your diet? Galatians 5:16-18 declares, "This I say then, Walk in the Spirit, and ye shall not fulfill the lust of the flesh. For the flesh lusteth against the Spirit, and the Spirit against the flesh: and these are contrary the one to the other: so that ye cannot do the things that ye would. But if ye be led of the Spirit, ye are not under the law."

Recalling the account found in the Book of Numbers Chapter 11, the children of Israel had their flesh conditioned to the food of Egypt. Egypt represents "bondage." They became accustomed to the food in the place of bondage. Now, as free people, they were complaining about the "manna" that God had provided for them. It did not taste as good to their fleshly appetite and therefore it was not their choice. This is like the experience of many believers who have spent time going back and forth into the world. The world's system and ways are just like Egypt. It is pure bondage. No person takes their first drink of alcohol and says "I want to be an alcoholic." No person says "I want to be addicted to pornography or drugs," or any other addictive habit or substance. Even so, bondages are still prevalent in the lives of unbelievers and, unfortunately, many believers as well. However, for believers, this need not be so! We have been set free and we are called to live in freedom, not bondage!

Body, Soul, and Spirit

Yet the struggle remains for many believers, and they are confused by their inner struggle. Some think that once a person is born again, these struggles should no longer exist. This issue plagues many believers today. However, we must realize that we are a trichotomous being, meaning that we have three parts: spirit (the "real us" that is regenerated when we are born again and which communes with God), soul (mind, will, and emotions), and body (physical).

John 3:5-6 states, "Jesus answered, Verily, verily, I say unto thee, except a man be born of water and of the Spirit, he cannot enter into the kingdom of God. That which is born of the flesh is flesh; and that which is born of the Spirit is spirit." Before we are born again, the body and soul "rule the house," so to speak. When our spirit is dead, in the pre-born again state, we are led by the desires of our body and soul. Before we are born again, we are in bondage, like the children of Israel were in Egypt. When the spirit of a person comes alive (is regenerated), we have a desire for God and the things of God, such as His Word and fellowship with Him. The problem is that we still have a body and mind that are conditioned to living in "Egypt" (bondage). Our spirit is alive and desires to do God's will, but our body and soul must "learn" to come into obedience to our spirit which is now in submission to the Holy Spirit. (Romans 12:1-2)

Conviction and Condemnation

Your spirit is the "real you." Many times believers get confused and live in condemnation because they feel an inner desire for their old lifestyle. They find themselves having an appetite for sin, the "food of Egypt". They know that they have been set free, just like the children of Israel were freed from bondage, but sometimes they long for the old diet that they had while in bondage. When you are born again, the "real you" desires to know and commune with God. Many believers live in confusion concerning this issue. Sometimes religion has brought condemnation to people because they still "struggle." However, I believe that a person's struggle is the evidence that he or she is indeed saved. Before they were saved, they didn't think twice about some of the things they did, and they did not feel "convicted." Conviction is the instrument that God uses to stop us from doing things, and "eating" things, that are destructive to us. Conviction brings with it the hope that there is always a way out! I Corinthians 10:13 declares, "There hath no temptation taken you but such as man can bear: but God is faithful, who will not suffer you to be tempted above that ye are able; but will with the temptation make also the way of escape, that ye may be able to endure it."

The difference between condemnation and conviction is that condemnation makes us feel like a failure and that there is no way out of the mess we are in. It makes us feel hopelessly guilty and unworthy. Conviction, on the other hand says, "Don't do that because it is harmful to you and your family. There is a better way. There is hope for you to change!" With conviction comes the hope of having the power to overcome the struggle, the certainty of forgiveness for the past, and the assurance of strength for the future.

Stand Fast and Persevere

Galatians 5:1 declares, "Stand fast therefore in the liberty wherewith Christ hath made us free, and be not entangled again with the yoke of bondage." Regarding the ongoing struggle, be encouraged by the truth that Christ has made us free! We are free from bondage and fear. We need no longer be controlled by worldly Egypt-like appetites. Still, the Apostle Paul teaches us (Galatians 5:1) that we have a responsibility to "stand fast." In the original Greek language this means to persevere! We have a responsibility to stand and fight, and to resist the temptations that the enemy tries to bring to us through our body and soul. Think of how many things we are bombarded with every week in the world that can tempt the appetites of the flesh. Billboards, magazines, television shows, popup ads on our computer screens, perhaps even a savvy accountant that encourages us to "cheat" on our taxes. Temptation comes in many forms and fashions, but we are admonished by Paul to persevere!

To "persevere" implies that one has strength! From where does our strength to stand come? Put very simply, our diet is the key to our strength. Just as a body builder must eat the right foods and maintain a strict diet if he or she wants to see results and build strength, a Christian must maintain a diet of "God's food" in order for their spirit and soul to see long lasting results! Recorded in John 6:51, Jesus said, "I am the living bread which came down from heaven, if any man eat of this bread, he shall live forever." Isaiah 40:31 encourages us that our strength will be renewed as we wait on God, as it declares, "But they that wait upon the LORD shall renew their strength; they shall mount up with wings as eagles; they shall run, and not be weary; and they shall walk, and not faint."

The Sun and the Poison

Even with the eagle's selective and strict diet, occasionally it will eat something that is poison. The eagle deals with this potentially deadly condition by lying on a rock ledge and staring intently into the sun until the sun rids its body of the poison. What a truth for us to consider! Though we never plan to do so, occasionally we ingest something that we then realize is poison! Whether we ingested it intentionally or not, we must eliminate it from our system. We can do so by staring at the "Son," putting our complete focus on Jesus, the Son of God. Hebrews 12:2-3 declares, "Looking unto Jesus the author and finisher of our faith; who for the joy that was set before him endured the cross, despising the shame, and is set down at the right hand of the throne of God. For consider him that endured such contradiction of sinners against himself, lest ye be wearied and faint in your minds." If you are struggling with a problem, addiction, or bondage, I encourage you to "focus on the Son" until you are whole.

John 1:1 states, "In the beginning was the Word, and the Word was with God, and the Word was God. John 1:14 declares, "And the Word was made flesh, and dwelt among us, (and we beheld his glory, the glory as of the only begotten of the Father), full of grace and truth." When God chose to communicate with humanity, which was separated from Him because of sin, He chose to send the Word, His Son! Jesus Christ is the Word of God. When we read, study, and meditate on the Word, we are in fact staring at the Son and ridding our mind of the poisons we occasionally ingest in the world.

How do we win the fight? Assume that there are two dogs. One has been fed a healthy diet, but the other hasn't eaten for several days. If those two dogs were to fight each other, which dog would win? Of course, the winner would be the dog who had been fed! In our daily life and walk with God, we will experience inner struggles. It may feel like part of us wants to do something that we know is wrong and contrary to God's Word. Whichever part of us has been fed is therefore stronger and will most likely win. Do we more often feed our fleshly desires and appetites or our spirit? Whichever "dog" we feed the most will win when the fight is on!

Perhaps studying our Bible will take on a different light if we think of it as our spiritual food and as an opportunity to communicate with Jesus. We should approach it as the Psalmist said—"meditate" on it. We should search it, study it, and use every word to persevere against the appetites of the flesh.

Perhaps you feel like you have been poisoned by being mistreated, cheated, lied about, or hurt. Perhaps you have gotten yourself into trouble by reverting back to the bondage diet of Egypt. Be encouraged, because you can look into God's Word and be cleansed. Psalm 119:9-10 declares, "Wherewith shall a young man cleanse his way? By taking heed thereto according to thy word. With my whole heart have I sought thee: Oh let me not wander from thy commandments." (ASV)

If you desire to possess greater strength, like the eagle you must become a selective, "finicky" eater. Don't just eat whatever is out there in the world. Most of it is dead. It will not satisfy or strengthen you, and it will not sustain you in the battles of life. Make up your mind to eat only those things which bring health, strength, and life to your spirit. Place your focus on Jesus, the Word of God.

CHAPTER 4

Like the Eagle in Renewal

The eagle is a highly habitual creature, and there are some things that the eagle does every day. One thing that is critical to the ongoing health and survival of the eagle is a daily practice called "preening." Preening is a process in which the eagle cleans and conditions its feathers one by one. Preening can take up to an hour. The eagle engages in this process by breathing on its feathers, which in effect "steam cleans" them. This process also seals the hairs in a feather together, creating a "zip-lock" effect on the feather. This helps prepare and equip the feathers for the "wear and tear" to which they will be subjected throughout the day because of the eagle's aggressive flying and hunting activities. During this process of preening, the eagle secretes a chemical from a gland that will waterproof the feathers. This is especially helpful, because much of the eagle's hunting is done by diving into the water to capture fish.

Daily Preening and Cleaning

The application of the preening process to a Christian's life is powerful. The eagle takes up to an hour to prepare for its day. We must understand the importance of spending time with the Lord as we face every new day.

Like the eagle cleans its feathers daily, we need to have our hearts and minds continually cleansed by the Lord. John 15:3 states, "Now ye are clean through the word which I have spoken unto you." The world is full of dirt and clutter. We are constantly exposed to the filth of sin, regardless of the intentions of our hearts, simply by living each day in this fallen, sin-soaked world. We can be driving down the road and see a billboard that causes us to think lustful thoughts. We receive emails that are not worth opening or viewing the attached video clip. Many times even jokes have a negative effect on us because at their root there is an underlying unscriptural message. Isaiah 52:11 declares, "...touch no unclean thing; go ye out of the midst of her; be ye clean, that bear the vessels of the Lord." God desires holiness in our lives. Spending time praying and studying the Word of God each morning will produce the result that John 15:3 promises. We need to be cleansed and prepared for the day. Just like the eagle produces a zip-lock effect on its feathers, the Word of God helps us to avoid, and not be influenced by, the filth all around us as we go through the day.

Psalm119:11 declares, "Thy word have I hid in mine heart, that I might not sin against thee." The Word has an inerrant power to cleanse us and keep us from sinning. The problems in which many people find themselves may not be as complex as they first appear. Most problems are a result of sin. Spending time in the Word each morning prepares us for a world in which we will be exposed to sin. Sometimes, the mentality and/or conversation of others around us is sinful. Subtly but consistently, day after day the effects of life without the Word allow uncleanness to enter into our thoughts, and it eventually works its way into our actions. Have you ever been around people who use foul language? At first, you are offended or taken back by their language. You wouldn't even consider using the words you hear. Then, subtly, the words may begin to creep into your speech, initially as an unintentional slip, then more consistently. It is much the same with things we see. At first we set a standard of not looking at things we know will lead to lustful thoughts. Then we begin to make exceptions one after another and suddenly we wonder, "Why am I so lustful? Where did these thoughts come from?" These are just a few examples of what happens to us when we don't preen and clean every day.

A number of years ago there was a fad, primarily among college students, in which they endeavored to determine how long they could go without showering. This practice was reported in the national news. I am unsure of the motive for this practice, but I can't imagine a fad where the goal is to be unclean and to emit a foul odor. However, it is analogous to how some Christians can become comfortable being "spiritually dirty."

Preening and cleaning is not a practice that we should do only after we have sinned. There is cleansing and forgiveness when we do fail, but spiritual preening and cleaning is a powerful preventive measure that we can practice daily to stay clean! Jesus said to pray that we would avoid temptation and sin, according to Matthew 6:13, which states, "And lead us not into temptation, but deliver us from evil…" I am thankful that we can be forgiven, but I am also thankful that we are empowered by God to resist the temptation to sin!

Rejuvenation

There is another practice, called rejuvenation, in which the eagle engages periodically. It senses instinctively when this practice is needed. Every eagle comes to a time in its life when its flight speed declines or its feathers give off a whistling sound during flight, which may alert its prey to the eagle's presence. In addition, the eagle may find that its talons and beak are not as sharp as they once were. When any of these conditions occur in the life of the eagle, it is time for the eagle to be renewed and rejuvenated. When the eagle reaches this point in its life, it immediately takes action. It flies up to a high place, as close to the sun as possible, and begins a process of rejuvenation.

In the first step of the process, the eagle begins to pluck off its feathers one by one. Some eagles find themselves totally devoid of feathers for up to 40 days before the new feathers grow back. The next thing the eagle will do is find a mountain stream in which to wash itself. The cold water in the stream removes dirt, parasites and lice from the eagle's skin. It also removes any feathers that are still adhering to the skin. Now totally cleansed, the eagle spends countless hours in the sun.

The eagle also addresses the problem of its dull talons and beak, which are critical to its hunting prowess. The eagle will find a rock on which it can sharpen its talons and beak by scraping them against the rock. This process can take hours and even days. Sometimes its talons are actually removed altogether to allow new sharp talons to grow back.

The eagle engages in daily preening, as well as periodic plucking, washing and grinding. Because of its faithful and consistent efforts, the eagle finds itself totally renewed at the end of this process. The eagle is in a sense "reborn" or reinstated to its youth with all of its vigor, power, speed and strength.

Every believer, leader, and minister can learn from this powerful example. God did not create the eagle to go on and on, flying, hunting, breeding, and building, without periodically being renewed and rejuvenated. The root of the word "recreation" is made up of two parts: the prefix "re-"and the word "create." It means "to create again; to become once again created." God has ordained a time of rest for every believer. This is not necessarily a time to be lazy, but rather a time to cease from normal activity and participate in the activity of rejuvenation. Of the Ten Commandments that God gave to Moses (Exodus 20), He elaborated the most on the observance of the Sabbath day. Exodus

20:8-11 states, "Remember the Sabbath day, to keep it holy. Six days shalt thou labour, and do all thy work: But the seventh day is the Sabbath of the LORD thy God: in it thou shalt not do any work, thou, nor thy son, nor thy daughter, thy manservant, nor thy maidservant, nor thy cattle, nor thy stranger that is within thy gates: For in six days the LORD made heaven and earth, the sea, and all that in them is, and rested the seventh day: wherefore the LORD blessed the Sabbath day, and hallowed it."

In this passage, God encouraged His people to set aside a day of rest in which they were instructed to cease from labor. The meanings of the word "holy" include "to be set aside, to be set apart, and to come out from among." This speaks to us of coming aside to rest, rejuvenate, and recreate. The principal reason many ministers leave the ministry is stress and burnout. Of all the Mosaic commandments, God had the most to say about remembering to set aside time to rest and rejuvenate. In our day and age, it is arguably the most violated of the commandments. It is critical that we periodically cease from our normal busy routine and set aside time to rest and be rejuvenated and renewed. Once again, we can learn from the eagle in this regard.

Close to the Son

The first step in spiritual rejuvenation is to come close to the Son. Like the eagle draws close to the sun in the natural, we must draw close to the Lord, spending time in His presence in worship and quiet meditation, listening for His voice. This in itself can be an incredible challenge. It may mean tuning out all kinds of distractions. Do you go through times of feeling overwhelmed, stressed, or burnt out on the job or at home? Consider taking a period of time when you can turn off your cell phone and escape from emails and all of the devices intended to improve communication and efficiency. These things often become traps for busyness that leave us sapped of a clear mind and a rested body.

It is said that the average business person spends up to six hours a day in activities involving the internet, email, and phone calls. Some of these activities do not even relate directly to business matters. There is a difference between business and busyness! How can we hear the voice of the Lord with so many other voices inundating our ears all of the time? The solution is simple. We must shut out everything else and draw close to Him. *Drawing close* to the Son is the first step in the rejuvenation process, and *staying close* to Jesus is the key element for the process to be effective. Isaiah 30:15 declares, "For thus saith the Lord GOD, the Holy One of Israel; In returning and rest shall ye be saved; in quietness and in confidence shall be your strength: and ye would not."

Lay Aside the Weight

The second vital step is when the eagle begins to pluck the feathers that are filled with dirt and parasites. Hebrews 12:1 states, "Wherefore seeing we also are compassed about with so great a cloud of witnesses, let us lay aside every weight, and the sin which doth so easily beset us, and let us run with patience the race that is set before us."

The writer of Hebrews discusses two distinct issues here: "every weight" and "the sin." Weight is not necessarily sin. Weight can be an activity that keeps us busy, masked in productivity, but which actually keeps us from being effective in life. Weight can be things that seem to be "good" but in the end they sap us of energy, time, and money. Weight can be thoughts of guilt, anxiety, or worry. Basically, we need a time to take inventory of our life to allow the Holy Spirit to show us areas that need to change. Sometimes we simply need to eliminate activity and thoughts that have been plaguing us and hindering our God-ordained purpose to soar to greatness. Weight can be relationships that are not God-ordained. We should not be rude to people or shun them, but we may need to distance ourselves from people that are draining us and not contributing to what God has called us to do. Being involved with, or "yoked to," certain people, may not be what God wants for us at certain times of our life. The Holy Spirit will be faithful to show us these areas that need repentance, which means to make a complete 180 degree turn and pursue a different direction. The "feather plucking" of the eagle is therefore symbolic of repentance in our lives.

Sin

Then there is the very real issue of sin. No matter who you are there are issues and areas where sin is most likely holding you back and bogging you down. Once again, the writer of Hebrews tells us to "cast off" these things, which means to throw them overboard and turn from them. The only things that God asks us to give up are things that may be hindering us, hurting us, or slowly destroying us. Sin is not only those things that we do which we know we should not do. (These are called *sins of commission*, because they are sins we *commit*). It is also sin to fail to do the things that we know we should do. (These are called *sins of omission* because they are things we *omit*).

In both cases, the Holy Spirit is the convicting agent. For most of us, it wouldn't take long to make a list of things that we do, no matter how minor, that we know we should not do, and also a list of things that we know we should be doing but which we are in fact not doing. These are all sins! Consider these words from John's first epistle and allow them to bring both conviction and hope. I John 1:8-10 declares, "If we say that we have no sin, we deceive ourselves, and the truth is not in us. If we confess our sins, he is faithful and just to forgive us our sins, and to cleanse us from all unrighteousness. If we say that we have not sinned, we make him a liar, and his word is not in us." These words convict us because they tell us that absolutely no one can say they have not, or do not, struggle with sin. We know that as we confess these sins, it is like plucking off old feathers that were slowing us down.

Like the eagle, at this point we find ourselves naked and exposed before God. Psalm 51:6 declares, "Behold, thou desirest truth in the inward parts: and in the hidden part thou shalt make me to know wisdom." Adam and Eve were created and placed in the garden naked. It was only after they sinned that they tried to cover their nakedness with fig leaves. Many people live their lives trying to cover themselves, instead of experiencing the recovery and restoration which comes through repentance.

Repentance

We must come close to the Son and repent! We must cast off, set aside, and eliminate every thought or action that is retarding our spiritual progress. God is faithful to forgive us and cleanse us, as His Word declares. God sees everything, so any attempt to cover up is futile. He sees us in our nakedness and loves us in spite of our weaknesses. Our weaknesses and sins cannot diminish God's love for us. He loves us and stands ready to forgive and help us off-load the weight that is heavy upon us. Jesus said," Come unto me, all ye that labour and are heavy laden, and I will give you rest." (Matthew 11:28). He did not say, "Come unto me and I will beat you with a big stick." He said that He will give us rest. It is tiring to carry around the burden of sin. We must allow Him to remove it from us today.

I invite you to pray this prayer with me. "Lord Jesus, I come to You today. I have areas in my life that are weighing me down

and burdening me. I have failed You and fallen short, but I repent. I give You my worries, my guilt, my shame, my insecuri-
ties, and my fear. Take it from me Lord, and give me rest. I ask
You to forgive me of _____ (fill in the blank)
and cleanse me from everything that causes me to disobey You.
Change me Lord, by Your power. I need to be renewed, rejuvenated, and filled with Your life in a fresh way today. I lay down
the things that You have shown me are weighing me down. With
Your help, I won't pick them up again. Thank You for making
me new, Jesus. Today is a new day because of You! Amen."

CHAPTER 5

Like the Eagle in Overcoming Storms and Serpents

Thus far, we have studied the characteristics of the eagle and how they parallel those that God requires of the believer. Exodus 19:4-5 declares that there is another perspective to consider, as it declares, "Ye have seen what I did unto the Egyptians, and how I bare you on eagles' wings, and brought you unto myself. Now therefore, if ye will obey my voice indeed, and keep my covenant, then ye shall be mine own possession from among all peoples: for all the earth is mine." In this passage, God draws an analogy between the eagle and Himself. We know from Genesis 1:26 that we were created in the image of God. God is the ultimate overcomer, having overcome even death itself. Therefore, as believers, we also inherently have these characteristics and the power to be overcomers.

Enemies of the Eagle: the Storm, and the Serpent

The Golden Eagle is one of the fastest, as well as the most powerful, majestic, and courageous of all birds. However, even this creature has enemies that can threaten its very life and existence. In this chapter, we will consider the two primary enemies of the eagle. One is the storm and the other is the serpent. The eagle learns how to survive the storm, and even uses the violent winds to carry it to new heights. The eagle also learns how to defeat and overcome the deadly serpent.

The Coming Storm

Violent storms can be deadly to the eagle if they are undetected. The key word is "undetected," because the eagle has an innate ability to sense when a storm is coming. The violent thermal updrafts which ground most birds and cause much of creation to scurry for cover serve as an opportunity for the eagle to soar. Using the powerful thermal updrafts, the eagle can fly into the eye of a storm, even a hurricane, reaching altitudes of up to 10,000 feet. Eagles have been observed almost motionless in hurricane force winds as they spread their wings and use the wind to climb higher.

Because of its magnificent vision, the eagle can spot a storm coming from great distances. Once it detects the approaching storm, it immediately prepares for it. The eagle, unlike many other creatures, will sit on the edge of its nest waiting for the onset of the storm. The eagle is seemingly unafraid, perhaps because it knows that it has what it takes to literally rise above the storm. The eagle will wait until the storm clouds approach, the velocity of the wind increases, and the rain begins to fall. At that point, it will launch itself into the wind. The eagle will stretch its wings and fly in a spiral motion, using each gust of wind as a power source to propel it higher and higher until it can see rays of sunlight. From an altitude high above the storm, it can look down and see the rain and the winds affecting everything below.

We have witnessed storms in a seemingly unprecedented manner in the past several years. They have hit the coasts and inland areas of Florida and many surrounding states. Hurricane Katrina had a devastating impact on New Orleans, Louisiana and all along the Gulf Coast of the United States. We are still haunted by the pictures of dead bodies and the survivors, some of whom were stranded for days in wretched conditions with very little, if any, food or water. Even though meteorologists predicted this storm and observed it as it approached, many people were unable to escape its ruthless power.

Sudden Storms

With modern technology and the science of meteorology, storms have become increasingly more predictable. However, in our lives, we are not always as aware of an impending "storm." We can sometimes be taken by surprise by circumstances and events in life. However, regardless of whether we see, or do not see, a storm approaching, God has equipped us with the necessary wisdom and power to get through storms by rising above them.

Storms can bring tremendous devastation. Often times a storm that arises suddenly will leave homes in shambles and city streets utterly destroyed. A storm can seem merciless as it destroys that which human beings have made with their hands. Interestingly, many of the people interviewed after hurricane Katrina were just thankful to be alive though they had lost all of their material possessions. Sometimes, a sudden storm may arise in our lives. Some people suddenly discover their spouse is having an affair. Some suddenly lose their job. Auto accidents, disease, and divorce are other examples of storms that can arise suddenly. I want to assure you that God is not surprised by any storm—*ever*.

Even if it appears as though things in your life have been destroyed, be assured that God is the great rebuilder and restorer. After Hurricane Katrina, people flocked to the devastated region to offer help. They worked tirelessly to rebuild homes and businesses. Some call it the "great American spirit," but I believe that rebuilding is an instinct that God put within us. If people who went through a horrible storm in the natural can rebuild homes and businesses, how much more can the God who breathed life into you in the beginning rebuild your life! If you are a victim of a storm that you simply could not escape, take heart. Not only can you survive the storms of life, but you can have everything in your life restored!

You Can Soar Above the Storm

John 16:33 declares, "These things I have spoken unto you, that in me ye might have peace. In the world ye shall have tribulation: but be of good cheer; I have overcome the world." Jesus intended these powerful words for all of us who must walk through life in a fallen world. If we read only the phrase about having tribulation in this world, we may become depressed. The Greek word translated "tribulation" means "trouble." The good news for the believer is that Jesus has overcome _every_ trouble and _every_ storm. He has made us to be more than conquerors, as Romans 8:37 declares, "Nay, in all these things we are more than conquerors through him that loved us."

The first key to overcoming is to know that God's Spirit was sent to lead us and guide us. As we walk closely with God, we will begin to sense when trouble is coming. Although sometimes trouble takes us totally off guard, on many other occasions we have an inner "knowing" about certain things. We sense that if we go in that direction, make that decision, connect with that person, or take that job, we will encounter "trouble." Has God ever "warned" you about something, or deep down you "had a feeling" and yet ignored it? Perhaps this happened concerning a relationship or a business deal, and, after ignoring the prompting of the Holy Spirit, you suddenly found yourself in trouble! Even if you ignored the warning and brought the trouble upon yourself because of poor choices, God will still give you the power to get out of that trouble. You can soar on the strength and power of His Spirit and He will help you out of every troublesome situation.

We must learn to be more sensitive to the still, small voice of God's Spirit within us. Even when we know that trouble is coming, or perhaps it has already arrived, we can rise above it. Like the eagle, we must begin to look at opposition, trouble and storms as opportunities to soar, to go to a higher place in God. When trouble comes, many people think only about surviving and somehow getting through it. However, in Romans 8:37, the Bible declares, "We are more than conquerors through Him that loved us." God wants us to begin to embrace the mentality of John 16:33. We need not be depressed, but instead we should be of good cheer. Why? Because we can soar above the storm by the power of prayer, God's Word, and His Holy Spirit.

Actively Waiting

At the beginning of a storm, we must emulate the eagle and simply be patient and trust the Lord. Isaiah 40:31 declares that, "But they that wait upon the Lord shall renew their strength; they shall mount up with wings as eagles; they shall run, and not be weary; and they shall walk, and not faint." This scripture teaches us that by waiting on the Lord, our strength will be renewed. When we think of the word "wait," we think of a passive state in which we are doing nothing. However, the Hebrew word *qavah*, which is translated "wait," carries a much different meaning. *Qavah* means "to expectantly bind, collect, or gather together, perhaps by twisting," and "to patiently look for, or tarry for, something or someone." It is not a passive word, but rather it is a word that denotes action.

To bind or twist together implies a coming together, a coming close, an intimacy. Therefore, to wait on the Lord is to actively obey everything the Word teaches us with regard to relationship with God. This includes the "activities" of worship, prayer, studying and meditating on God's Word. We must come close to Him by spending time with Him. At the onset of a storm we can confidently approach and worship Him, which brings His presence into our lives and situation. We can pray, which is a dialogue between us and God. In prayer, we can give God our fear, doubt, hurt, disappointment, and unbelief, and He gives us love, faith, healing, hope and confidence about the future.

Note that the eagle continues to fly above the storm until he can see the rays of the sun! We must learn to press into God through the darkness, confusion, fear, and shock of a troubling time. If we continue to press into Him, we will eventually see the light of the Son! There is a time to wait, be still, and stand! Ephesians 6:13-14 declares, "Wherefore take unto you the whole armour of God, that ye may be able to withstand in the evil day, and having done all, to stand. Stand therefore, having your loins girt about with truth, and having on the breastplate of righteousness."

We learn from the eagle that motion (activity) at the wrong time is not necessarily the right action to take. We have all been in a frantic situation in which someone yells, "Don't just stand there, do something!" Ephesians 6:13-14, as well as the example of the eagle, insist the opposite: "Don't just do something, stand there!" Timing is very important. There is a time when the best thing to do is stand, wait, worship, and pray. Many times, we feel that we need to be doing something, but we often react out of emotion instead of waiting for God to speak to us. There will come a time for action, a time to launch out and do something. Until you discern that moment, wait on Him!

Determined To Fly

The eagle is determined to fly. While other creatures are threatened by stormy winds, the eagle sees them as an opportunity to go higher. He lives in launch mode! Many people go into "cave" mode when they are facing a storm. They want to hide, self-medicate, sleep, or find some other way to ignore the storm. None of these are effective because they don't bring us closer to the Son! The eagle has an innate knowledge that the storm cannot hurt him because he has the ability to rise above it. _As believers, we must become absolutely persuaded and convinced without a doubt that God will see us through!_ Romans 4:21 declares, "And being fully persuaded that, what he had promised, he was able also to perform." Romans 8:38-39 states, "For I am persuaded, that neither death, nor life, nor angels, nor principalities, nor powers, nor things present, nor things to come, nor height, nor depth, nor any other creature, shall be able to separate us from the love of God, which is in Christ Jesus our Lord."

Knowing that God has equipped us to overcome any storm and go higher, we need not fear any circumstance we face in life. Isaiah 54:17 declares, "No weapon that is formed against thee shall prosper; and every tongue that shall rise against thee in judgment thou shalt condemn. This is the heritage of the servants of the LORD, and their righteousness is of me, saith the LORD." God has given us overcoming power. When the storms of life come, we must not hide, but instead look for the opportunity to soar. God is going to take us higher!

Toward the Son

Please note that the eagle's direction is toward the sun. Whenever we have a doubt in a situation or circumstance, we must move toward the Son by getting into God's Word and into His presence through prayer and worship. Sometimes, this means seeking out men or women that we know have a deep relationship with the Lord and who will give us Godly counsel and, most importantly, will earnestly pray for us.

When I was a young boy, just 2 ½ years of age, the doctors told my parents that I had pneumonia in both lungs and I would not live. In those days, medicine wasn't as advanced as it is today. Doctors surgically inserted a tube into my back to drain the fluid from my lungs. It was all they could do to delay impending death. My parents, who had tried everything they knew to do, saw an advertisement in a newspaper of a small storefront church that believed in divine healing. As a last desperate measure, they carried me to the church where the pastor prayed and asked God to give me a new set of lungs. By God's grace, I was miraculously and instantaneously healed! The doctor confirmed that the fluid in my lungs had completely stopped draining so he removed the drainage tube, stating as a result that I was either going to die or a miracle had occurred. Well, thanks be to God, I didn't die in that storm, but instead I soared above it. My parents got saved and God raised me up by His power and I went on to preach for over five decades and I am still preaching today. With my little dying body in their arms, my parents moved toward the Son!

I believe that God will give us specific direction in a storm if we will wait on Him. If we are obedient to His voice, we will soar above the storm. God will open a door or a window, or He will part a surging river. Something will change, and we will know that even though the storm is still raging, we are soaring above it, close to the Son! Soaring is a condition of our spirit and attitude, and is not dependent on how the circumstances appear. Everything can look bad, dark, stormy, and gloomy, but we are soaring because we know that no weapon formed against us shall prosper. We know that we are more than conquerors, and we know that God is faithful to perform all that He has promised. Although the storm may seem endless, He will give us strength by His Spirit to continue to soar. We will go higher. The next time a storm rolls in, I encourage you to say to yourself, "This is an opportunity to soar higher and grow closer to Jesus!"

Maturity and Endurance

There is another truth about the eagle in the storm that we can learn from Isaiah 40:30-31, which declares, "Even the youths shall faint and be weary, and the young men shall utterly fall: But they that wait upon the LORD shall renew their strength; they shall mount up with wings as eagles; they shall run, and not be weary; and they shall walk, and not faint." This passage says that the youth will faint! I don't think the writer here is referring to chronological age. The analogy certainly rings true that young people seem to have more energy, almost endless energy, but I believe that the deeper truth here is about "maturity." The immature can be great starters but weak finishers. It is not how we start the race but how we finish that is important!

We develop the ability to endure storms by living according to the Word and trusting in the Lord. All believers need endurance to withstand a storm of any duration. There are many times in life that the nights seem longer than the days. In these moments, we need the power of the Holy Spirit to endure. As long as the wind is blowing, the eagle can spread his wings and stay in the air. Likewise, no matter how bad or how long the storm is, we can endure it!

Don't Quit, Be Renewed

Here is a truth that may seem too simplistic or obvious, but it is important. *Don't quit! Don't give up!* The Apostle Paul wrote to his spiritual son Timothy, "I have fought a good fight, I have finished my course, I have kept the faith: henceforth there is laid up for me the crown of righteousness, which the Lord, the righteous judge, shall give to me at that day; and not to me only, but also to all them that have loved his appearing." (II Timothy 4:7-8). Paul was able to declare that he "finished his course." In this life, our course is not always easy. In fact, Paul's course was filled with persecution, trials, beatings, and imprisonment, but he did not quit! I encourage you to remember that mature eagles *never* give up, even though the storm may last for a seemingly endless period of time.

Unless we are renewed, we constantly feel tired, weary, and worn out. Many people in our fast-paced, stressful society are simply exhausted. People whom I meet all over the country are weary from the pressures and storms of life. The effects are seen in marriages because people are too tired to show love to one another. The effects are seen in families because parents are too tired to get involved in the lives of their children. Even though people are working diligently, many are dissatisfied with their jobs. Normally the cause of the dissatisfaction or discontentment isn't the job itself. Rather, because they are not refreshed and renewed, their creativity and energy to do the job is gone. "Quit" is written all over their faces. The key to being renewed is in the presence of the Lord. Sometimes the most practical thing we can do is set some time aside and get away, even for just a day. Sometimes we think that we must spend many hours in a church service to get everything right with God. That is just not true. Some people are even deceived into thinking that they are too busy to spend time with God. That is the biggest mistake that we can make because His presence is the place where we are renewed, rejuvenated, recharged, recreated, and "re-lifed."

Even one half hour daily with God can bring refreshing and renewal. I encourage you to make time daily to be with the Lord, to be in His presence, to talk to Him and let Him talk to you. As a result, you will find renewed strength to carry you through the pressures of life. You will no longer feel "worn out," or feel like you want to "crash land" or quit. Instead of quitting, try soaring! Get away, take some time…take a day, or even an hour, and get with God. You will be renewed. You will have strength to make it through every storm and you will finish your course!

The Deadly Serpent

The serpent is another enemy of the eagle, and the serpent represents man's enemy as well. It was the devil, in the form of a serpent, who came and deceived mankind. In Genesis 3:14, God declared that a curse would exist, an enmity between the woman's seed (Jesus) and the serpent (Satan). Genesis 3:14-15 states, "And Jehovah God said unto the serpent, Because thou hast done this, cursed art thou above all cattle, and above every beast of the field; upon thy belly shalt thou go, and dust shalt thou eat all the days of thy life: and I will put enmity between thee and the woman, and between thy seed and her seed: he shall bruise thy head, and thou shalt bruise his heel." Luke 10:19 declares, "Behold, I give unto you power to tread on serpents and scorpions, and over all the power of the enemy: and nothing shall by any means hurt you." It is clear that the serpent appeared as a spiritual enemy of mankind.

Similarly, the serpent is a natural enemy of the eagle. The serpent is perhaps the only creature in the animal kingdom that can harm or kill the eagle if it does not react to the serpent's attacks in a timely and proper manner.

The eagle keeps its eggs warm for up to forty days before they hatch. The baby eaglets are formed in the egg and they have one tooth which they use to break through the egg. They are not aided by anything on the outside, but rather they are born with all they need to break through the shell of the egg. The serpent comes instinctively either just before the eaglets are to be born or right after their birth to try to destroy the eggs or devour the young eaglets. The snake is subtle and will try to get into the nest undetected. This is a difficult task because the mother and baby eaglet are on the lookout, but occasionally the serpent will slither in undetected.

The Serpent Attacks

Baby eaglets instinctively screech at the arrival of the serpent, and this sounds the alarm for the mother eagle to take action. The mother eagle will go directly at the serpent and defend her young in one of three ways. If the serpent is trying to strike the eaglet, the mother eagle will offer her breastbone for the serpent to strike. Although she does not have a natural immunity against the serpent's venom, her breastbone will often deflect the attack, and though she is wounded, she can avoid death.

Secondly, the mother eagle will go on the offensive. She will use her beak to repeatedly bite and stab the serpent until it is dead. Thirdly, the eagle may grab onto the serpent with her powerful talons and carry it away from the nest. The eagle will fly with the serpent in her talons until she spots a rock or the edge of a cliff. The eagle, while flying at a high rate of speed, will smash the serpent against the rock. The serpent will either die from the impact of the rock, or from the impact of falling to the ground below.

These attributes of the serpent and the eagle illustrate many truths about the battle between mankind and our enemy, Satan. We must realize that the serpent is subtle. The enemy of our soul is constantly attempting some tactic that we don't expect. Young believers are often led into temptation as the enemy places temptations in front of them that look appealing yet in the end will bring only pain and destruction.

I John 2:16 states, "For all that is in the world, the lust of the flesh, and the lust of the eyes, and the pride of life, is not of the Father, but is of the world." The serpent is aware that the lust of the flesh (our sinful nature), the lust of the eyes (our appetites), and pride are three areas into which he can subtly lead us if we are not watchful and aware of what he is doing.

The lust in our sinful nature is continually a target of the enemy for our destruction. There are many lusts of which we must be constantly aware: the lust for power, sex, money, fame, and self gratification, to name but a few.

Pride and Humility

Pride is another area in which the serpent trips up and traps many people. Pride is the false notion that man can "make it" independent of God. Pride is man-centered, man-dependent, and God-absent. As the Word of God declares in Proverbs 16:18, "Pride goeth before destruction, and an haughty spirit before a fall." The way to avoid a proud heart and haughty spirit is to continually humble ourselves.

I Peter 5:5 declares, "Likewise, ye younger, submit yourselves unto the elder. Yea, all of you be subject one to another, and be clothed with humility: for God resisteth the proud, and giveth grace to the humble." Matthew 18:4 states, "Whosoever therefore shall humble himself as this little child, the same is greatest in the kingdom of heaven." Matthew 23:12 declares, "And whosoever shall exalt himself shall be abased; and he that shall humble himself shall be exalted." James 4:10 states, "Humble yourselves in the sight of the Lord, and he shall lift you up."

From these scriptures we learn an important lesson: we will either humble ourselves or we will be humbled. Matthew effectively tells us that those who exalt themselves or are proud, independent of God and self-reliant, will be abased or brought low (humbled). James tells us that if you humble yourself, God will lift you up. Peter communicates the truth that God will actually resist those that refuse to humble themselves, but God will give grace and strength to those that choose to humble themselves. The choice is simple—we can either humble ourselves or be humbled!

To be humble is to acknowledge the Lordship of Jesus in our life. Humility is looking to Him, continually leaning on Him and acknowledging that we cannot save ourselves or navigate through this life without God. Humility is truly an attitude of the heart. Humility is not weakness. As a matter of fact, when we put ourselves in that place of humility before God, we will be strong and confident in the grace and strength that He gives us.

Offering the Sacrifice

The enemy targets the young and the newly born. It is interesting that the serpent attacks eaglets just before, or just after, their birth. Satan attacks marriages that have just been formed, businesses that have just been started, and churches that have just been planted. The serpent (enemy) sees the potential of a powerful future and he wants to destroy it at the onset, before it has a chance to grow and be productive.

It is a beautiful thing that the mother eagle offers her breastbone against the strikes of the serpent. We know that Jesus offered His body as a sacrifice for us. The soldiers at the cross pierced His side, according to John 19:34. The serpent thought that he was striking a final blow at Jesus, but the thrust of the spear released His pure uncontaminated blood which flowed to provide our salvation and wholeness. Jesus endured the serpent's attack, and in so doing, He took our sin upon Himself. By that act, He fulfilled the promise of Genesis 3:15 that the Seed (Jesus) would crush the serpent's head.

The Lord Jesus Christ offered Himself as a sacrifice. He stood between us and the serpent and endured the whipping, beating, nailing, and piercing—every attempt the enemy made to destroy Him. Like the powerful mother eagle, Jesus stood between us and the serpent, and now we live because He lives! Jesus declared in John 14:19, "Because I live, you will live also." (NASB) Through Him, we have overcome the serpent!

The Power in the Mouth

The mother eagle takes its beak and strikes at the serpent repeatedly until the serpent becomes lifeless. The beak is symbolic of our mouth. We have the Word of God that we can use against the serpent. We can strike him back by speaking the Word of God, and in that Word we have power and authority. Proverbs 18:21 declares, "Death and life are in the power of the tongue: and they that love it shall eat the fruit thereof." Romans 10:10 states, "For with the heart man believeth unto righteousness; and with the mouth confession is made unto salvation." Romans 10:8 declares, "The word is near you, even in your mouth and in your heart; that is, the word of faith which we proclaim."

The Word of God is like the beak of the eagle. When we spend time studying, memorizing, and meditating on it, the Word becomes a powerful weapon against the enemy and it can literally become the difference between life and death. We can use His Word any time the enemy comes against us. Regardless of what the enemy brings our way, the Word has an answer, and if we keep the Word in our heart and in our mouth, it becomes the weapon that will destroy the serpent in every situation.

The key is to speak the Word, not just to know it. When the enemy throws sickness at us, we have I Peter 2:24 which declares, "Who his own self bare our sins in his own body on the tree, that we, being dead to sins, should live unto righteousness: by whose stripes ye were healed." If the enemy throws fear at us, we have II Timothy 1:7, which states, "For God hath not given us the spirit of fear; but of power, and of love, and of a sound mind." The enemy cannot destroy our dreams, vision, or future when we fight him with the Word of God.

Smashing the Serpent on the Rock

Sometimes the eagle picks up the serpent and smashes it on a rock. Matthew 21:42 states, "Jesus said to them, "Did you never read in the Scriptures, `The stone which the builders rejected, this became the chief corner stone; this came about from the Lord, and it is marvelous in our eyes'?" (NASB) Acts 4:11-12 declares, "He is the stone which was rejected by you, the builders, but which became the chief corner stone; and there is salvation in no one else; for there is no other name under heaven that has been given among men by which we must be saved." (NASB)

Jesus is the Rock upon which the enemy has been smashed. The serpent thought he could slither into, and destroy, the plan of God. He thought that by crucifying Jesus he would annihilate humanity and terminate mankind's potential reconciliation with God. What he did not realize was that in that moment, like the eagle that grabs the serpent with its talons, God took the serpent and smashed him against the Rock, Christ Jesus!

The next time the enemy slithers up to you and tempts you, persecutes you, or tries to bring depression on you, remember that he has already been smashed against the Rock, Jesus Christ. God saw to it that we, His children (eaglets), would live! Because the serpent has been smashed, he has no power over us!

CHAPTER 6

Like the Eagle in Commitment

The word "commitment" almost seems like a four-letter word in our self-absorbed, self-focused "What's in it for me?" society. Many people move from relationship to relationship or from job to job, constantly seeking something that they feel would benefit themselves to a greater degree. Commitment means "to pledge or obligate oneself to do or be something." It infers staying dedicated to a person or a task or cause through both the good times and the bad times. It means not running away, quitting, or bailing out when times get tough. Commitment can be difficult, distasteful, and even repulsive to our flesh because it requires us to look past our own needs and desires in pursuit of the greater good.

With regard to commitment, the eagle once again stands out among the creatures in the animal kingdom. Nearly all creatures possess instincts for mating and reproduction. However, the eagle is quite remarkable in that it goes far beyond just the physical act of mating, and exhibits a remarkable lifelong commitment to its chosen mate. In this chapter, we will learn how eagles create a strong and lasting lifetime bond in their mating relationship, and how we can become "like the eagle" in commitment.

Why is Commitment So Difficult?

Our natural human tendency is toward ourselves and our personal comfort and convenience, rather than toward commitment. We tend to want to be committed only on our own terms. That is, our flesh wants to define the boundaries and limitations of our commitment to God, a relationship, job, task, or calling. Commitment requires a conscious choice of our will, and is difficult because it:

- makes demands upon us,
- challenges our priorities,
- invades our personal space and privacy, and
- deprives us of selfish pleasures.

Commitment and Maturity

Commitment is closely related to maturity. Young children frequently use the words "me" and "mine" and are very focused on their own comfort, needs, possessions, and desires. Sadly, though, just because someone is physically mature doesn't mean that they don't act or think childishly. Even as adults, we can all too often think in an immature and childish manner, demanding our own way on our own terms and in our own timeframe, with little or no regard to God's will or anyone else's wants or needs.

As believers, it is important that we make a conscious decision to be mature in our thinking. We must strive to be committed in our personal relationship with God, and we should also be committed to the things that He loves. His highest priority is people, and we should be lovers, servants, givers, and blessers, at the cost of our personal comfort or desires. Something else that God loves is His church, and it is important for every one of us as believers to commit ourselves to being an active and contributing member of a church family. (Hebrews 10:24-25)

The Young Eagle

When the eagle is about one year old, he leaves the security of his parents' nest, strikes out on his own, and begins to take care of himself. Although he has been taught well by his parents, he still has much to learn about being an eagle. Flying, hunting, and courting are three of the things that will occupy much of his time as a young eagle. About three years after the eagle has been on his own, he begins to instinctively feel the need to be joined with another eagle. He takes an interest in another eagle, and begins a process of courting.

This may start with a game of "tag" that could last for days. Eventually, the female eagle becomes bored and she begins to play another game, one that eagles have instinctively been playing for hundreds of years. In this game, the female dives to the ground and grasps a small stick in her talons. She then ascends high into the sky while the male follows close behind in pursuit. When she reaches an altitude of 8,000 to 10,000 feet, she begins to fly in a "figure eight" pattern of wide circles and curves. The male eagle follows closely behind. Suddenly, the female drops the stick. The male breaks the pattern and immediately dives at a high rate of speed in order to catch the stick for her. He attempts to return the stick to the female, but she feigns disinterest and, instead of accepting the stick, she dives back to the ground to find a larger stick.

The male eagle returns the small stick to the ground and again closely follows the female, who is again ascending with the slightly larger stick, this time to an altitude of 6,000 to 8,000 feet. The eagles repeat the same actions as before, and the game continues. Each time, she goes for an increasingly larger stick, and each time she flies a little lower and a little faster before intentionally dropping the stick. Each time, the male swoops to catch the stick, and if he ever misses it, the female flies off and won't play the game with him anymore. The game reaches its climax when the female is flying at a high rate of speed in a tight figure eight about 500 feet above the ground. At this stage of the game, the stick is actually a small log that weighs nearly as much as she does. She drops it and expects the male to catch this large, heavy log without crashing into the ground. For his sake, and the sake of the relationship, he had better catch that stick!

Sky-High Commitment

The eagles' courtship takes place in the sky, where the eagle is most at ease. Their very best flight skills and maneuvers, surprisingly, are reserved for displays of affection. Some have even been observed to perform a "loop the loop" maneuver, which is very difficult aerodynamically. The male and female eagles soar and dive together in a breathtaking display of power and agility. They gradually begin to interlock in flight, engaging in amazing aerial maneuvers and rolling somersaults. While they fly, they sing "love songs" and make "love calls" that echo throughout their domain.

As they play the game of "drop the stick," at some point the male will dive at the female and she will roll on her back in mid-air, flashing her deadly talons at the male. This is not an act of hostility, but rather it is a sign of love, as they are literally reaching out to one another. The two eagles clasp talons and, while locked together, they engage in a series of rolls and cartwheels as they plummet toward earth. This is a symbol of complete and total trust in one another, even at the risk of death.

A Strong and Lasting Bond

Although the eagles' initial courtship flights take place while they are in the courting and mating stage of their lives, many eagle couples continue to perform this ritual of love regularly throughout their lifetimes as a sign of devotion and affection. It serves to strengthen their bond of love and commitment to each other. The bond between the eagles is very strong and grows stronger throughout the years. A mated eagle couple will rarely fight, and they are genuine friends who are happy in each other's company. They take time to soar and to hunt together. Often while the female sits on the nest, the male will gently groom her and stroke her feathers. The male may even "baby sit" the eggs at times, and he will commit to raising the eaglets alone should anything happen to his mate. That is true commitment and dedication.

During times of adversity, the eagle couple will come together as one unified front. They work together to care for and protect their family against anything that threatens to harm them. They are a tremendous example of two becoming one, setting aside their own selfish desires for the greater good. Oh that we as humans would learn from the eagle's example of commitment in our marriages and relationships!

The Ultimate Example of Commitment

God Himself is the ultimate example of commitment. He cares for us so deeply that He sent Jesus Christ, His only Son, to come to earth and sacrifice His life for us. Giving one's life is the most noble and selfless thing that a person can do for another, and the ultimate example of love and commitment. Jesus declared, "Greater love has no one than this, that he lay down his life for his friends" (John 15:13 NIV) and He displayed His love as He went to the cross just hours after making that statement to His disciples. Romans 5:8 states, "But God demonstrates his own love for us in this: While we were still sinners, Christ died for us." (NIV) Jesus loves us so much that He gave His life for us before we even knew we needed a Savior!

We were created by God in His image and, as born again believers, we should be excellent examples of commitment. The Spirit of God lives within us, and as we dedicate ourselves to knowing Him and serving Him, we become more and more like Him. We begin to have God's heart of love, grace, and mercy toward people. We begin to look past our own needs, and we have a desire to meet the needs of others. Jesus referred to His disciples as servants, friends, and even brothers, and that is what we should be. We must have a passion to be people of sacrifice, servanthood, relationship, and commitment. As we allow the Spirit to change our hearts, we become better husbands or wives, parents, friends, and employees because we desire to fulfill God's plan for our lives and be examples of His love and commitment to the world. As we become more and more like Him, we look to be a blessing to others rather than just being consumed with our own needs and desires.

How Is Your Commitment Level?

I encourage you to take a moment and examine your heart, your attitude, and your lifestyle. Are you "like the eagle" in commitment? Allow the Holy Spirit to reveal to you the thoughts, attitudes, and actions that are self-centered and immature. Look closely at your relationships, your work ethic, and even the way you pray. Are many of your prayers self-centered and self-focused? Are you a person that others view as devoted, dedicated, and committed to the things that really matter in life? If you fall short in any of these areas, as we all do from time to time, it's not too late to repent (which means to make a 180 degree turn and go in the opposite direction) and become a person of commitment. As you spend time with the Lord, His Spirit will mold you and shape you into someone who is like the eagle, and more importantly, like God Himself, in commitment. Be resolved and steadfast like Joshua, who declared, "...choose you this day whom ye will serve...but as for me and my house, we will serve the LORD." (Joshua 24:15)

CHAPTER 7

Becoming Like the Eagle

Deep down in every human heart, I believe there is an inner "knowing" that there is more to life than what we see, feel, and experience. God clearly confirms this in Ecclesiastes 3:11 which declares, "...He has also set eternity in the hearts of men." (NIV) I believe that we all desire to live a life that has meaning and purpose, a life that truly will echo in eternity. Unfortunately, the harsh realities of living in a sin-soaked world tend to beat us down and attempt to steal our purpose and our noble dreams. Too many people live day to day just trying to survive. Like Solomon, they run from thing to thing, person to person, activity to activity, job to job, or church to church, trying to find something that satisfies their innermost longings. They know that there is an eagle on the inside of them, but life has relegated them to living like a vulture (feeding off dead things) or a chicken (constantly pecking at the ground).

There is only one way to escape this life of frustration and futility. There is only one way to accomplish the purpose for which you were created. There is only one way to live a visionary, strong, purposeful, committed, overcoming life, like that of the eagle's. The one way is to enter into a personal relationship with the God who created you. If your heart is stirred and you are inspired as you observe the noble and majestic lifestyle of the eagle, and you want to experience that kind of life for yourself, I have good news for you. In fact, I have the best news you have ever heard. God loves you and wants you to live a victorious life, and He wants you to live with Him in a perfect place, where there are no storms, no serpents, no weariness, no tears, and no darkness...forever!

God made a way for you to be accepted and welcomed into His presence and to receive the gift of eternal life. None of us deserve this gift and we are all utterly unworthy of it. We are all imperfect, and we have all sinned. Romans 3:23 declares, "For all have sinned, and come short of the glory of God." Because we are all sinners and are therefore imperfect, God made a way for us to become "perfect" in His sight. He is truly perfect, and sin (imperfection) cannot live in His presence. However, there is One who is perfect, who lived a sinless life and came to earth for the express purpose of sacrificing His life, taking our sins upon Himself, and dying on a cross. Of course, I am talking about Jesus Christ. He freely laid down His own life, and in doing so, He opened up the doors to heaven for all of us.

Romans 10:9-10 states, "That if thou shalt confess with thy mouth the Lord Jesus, and shalt believe in thine heart that God hath raised him from the dead, thou shalt be saved. For with the heart man believeth unto righteousness; and with the mouth confession is made unto salvation." Verse 13 declares, "For whosoever shall call upon the name of the Lord shall be saved." The invitation is for "whosoever," and that includes you!

When we believe in Jesus Christ, repent of our sins, and receive Him as our Lord and Savior, God the Father declares us forgiven and receives us into His family. God no longer sees our guilt and sin when He looks upon us, but rather He sees the blood of Jesus, the perfect spotless Lamb, and it is enough to wash our sins away, and we are born again. God makes us a new creation in Christ (II Corinthians 5:17) and He commits Himself to walk with us through every high and hard place in life.

His Holy Spirit comes to live inside of us, and He is our constant comforter, teacher, and guide. God is more committed to you than you are to yourself, and He will go to any length (such as dying on the cross) to prove it to you. I encourage you right now, if you have never been born again, to search your heart for the gentle tug of God's Spirit as He invites you to become part of His family forever.

I encourage you to pray to Him right now along these lines: "Jesus, I come to You just as I am. I acknowledge that I am a sinner, and I have fallen short in so many ways. But I believe that You love me, You died on the cross for me, and You rose from the dead to give me new life. I repent of my sins, Jesus. Please forgive me, and wash me clean. Give me a new start in life, and help me to please You and fulfill Your purpose for me here on the earth. Thank You for being eternally committed to me. Thank You for loving me, Jesus, and for giving me the incredible gift of eternal life, and the privilege of spending eternity in heaven with You, where there will be no more tears, no more pain, no more storms, no more serpents, and no more death. I love you Jesus, and I surrender my life to You, Lord. Thank You for saving my soul and filling me with Your Holy Spirit. Draw me close to You, and help me to grow closer to You each and every day. Amen."

If you prayed that prayer in the sincerity of your heart, you are a new person in Christ! You may still experience "storms and serpents" while here on the earth, but you will be able to reach out and take hold of Jesus' hand, and together you will soar above them and come out victoriously. God bless you as you begin your new life in Christ!

END NOTES

1 "Near to the Heart of God" words and music by Cleland B. McAfee, 1903 public domain

2 "Wind Beneath My Wings" composed by Jeff Silvar and Larry Henley

REFERENCES

Soaring with Eagles: Principles of Success by Bill Newman
Toowong, Australia: Bill Newman Intl, 1994

The Eagle Christian by Kenneth Price
Old Faithful Publishing Company, 1994

Zondervan Pictorial Encyclopedia of the Bible General Editor Merrill C. Tenney
Zondervan, 1975

The Merriam-Webster Dictionary
Merriam-Webster, 2005

More Inspirational Books from Pastor Leonard Gardner

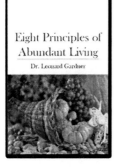

Eight Principles of Abundant Living

In this inspiring and thought provoking book, Pastor Gardner examines each recorded miracle in the Book of John to uncover spiritual principles of abundant living which can lead you into a lifestyle of deep satisfaction, joy, fulfillment, and true happiness.

The Unfeigned Love of God

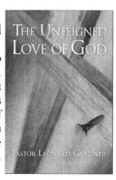

The Bible uses the word "unfeigned" to characterize the indescribable love of God. Unfeigned means "genuine, real, pure, not pretentious, and not hypocritical." This powerful book, derived from a series of sermons by Pastor Gardner, will help you understand, accept, and embrace the incredible love God seeks to lavish on you.

Walking Through the High and Hard Places

Life has its ups and downs. The key to a fulfilling life is learning to "walk through" whatever situation or circumstance you encounter, and to emerge victoriously! The spiritual principles you learn in this book will give you the strength to handle any circumstance in life!

The Work of the Potter's Hands

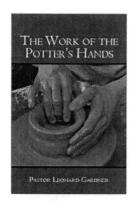

You are not alive by accident! Isaiah 64:8 declares that God is the potter, and we are the clay. This book examines seven types of Biblical pottery vessels and the process the potter uses to shape and repair vessels. Learn powerful life lessons and know your life is in the hands of a loving God who is forming you through life's experiences so that you "take shape" to fulfill your unique purpose.

It's All in the Blood

This fascinating book draws intriguing and powerful analogies between the incredible design and operation of blood in the human body, and the life-changing spiritual power and provision that is available in the blood of Jesus Christ.

Liberating Word Ministries

www.liberatingword.org

COMING SOON FROM PASTOR LEONARD GARDNER:

In This Manner (Principles of Prayer)

The Blood Covenant

Hearing God

Chosen to Follow Jesus

Greater Than the Gates

Hindrances to Spiritual Growth

The Planting of the Lord

Contact Pastor Gardner to:
- receive his free monthly newsletter;
- schedule him for a ministry meeting at your church;
- or order his books or other resources.

Liberating Word Ministries
Pastor Leonard Gardner
PO Box 380291
Clinton Township, MI 48038

Phone: (586) 216-3668
Fax: (586) 416-4658
lgardner@liberatingword.org

2487776

Made in the USA